THE
ENTREPRENEURS'
TOOLKIT
FOR SUCCESS

VOLUME 1

Produced by the Founders of Hey Taxi

Dawn Cermak and Jill Knerr

Edited by Lil Barcaski

Published by: GWN Publishing
www.GWNPublishing.com

Cover Design: Jose Diacono Jr.

ISBN: 978-1-959608-24-0

DEDICATION

This book is dedicated to all of the brave, resourceful, mission-driven female entrepreneurs who are committed to taking control of their destiny, and following their dreams!

TABLE OF CONTENTS

INTRODUCTION

Publishing our own book has been a goal for *Hey Taxi* since our inception. We are not only avid readers, but also huge fans of learning from our peers to fast track our own success. So, a compilation book that shares the stories and success tips from other mission-driven female entrepreneurs was the perfect combination of allowing you, our readers, to expand both your network and your knowledge base to help you build and scale your own profitable business.

As female entrepreneurs, we wear ALL the hats—accounting, marketing, sales, public relations, operations... the list is endless. And we all have to admit we do not love wearing every hat.

What we enjoy doing most, and where we shine the brightest, is when we are focused in our own Zone of Genius. The tasks and knowledge that come to us so easily and also bring us fulfillment when we focus in that space. The best way to focus our talents to achieve the maximum ROI is to outsource the rest of the work to those whose Zones of Genius cover our weak spots!

We did not start out on our business journey with all the answers, nor do our combined skillsets cover all the areas to run a successful business. But what we have done right is to connect with so many amazing and accomplished women in the past two (going on three) years whose own expertise and generosity have played a key role in where we are today with building and scaling *Hey Taxi*. From financial experts to social media gurus to graphic designers to sales funnel pros (God Bless them all!), we have sought out and contracted their talents to move the needle in our business in all the areas where we readily admit our personal shortcomings or lack of desire to become experts in those fields.

Hey Taxi and *The Entrepreneurs' Toolkit for Success* are both vehicles designed to give you that support, that knowledge and that community as well as the tools, and network to build and scale your own profitable legacy business.

Now, we invite you to read on and learn from your peers—each has a very different business focus and personal story as well as key tips they have used to find success against any odds or challenges they have faced. We know you will find inspiration, comradery, and practical, take-away knowledge you can apply today to help boost your own business going forward. Plus the expert resources of these authors whom you can now leverage to support your own business.

At *Hey Taxi*, we believe in **TAKING ACTION**, so remember, each chapter has a **LINK** for you to connect with the author directly and take that needed step in the right direction.

As always...
To Your Success,
Dawn and Jill, Your Hey Taxi Founders

I want to be a part of your journey as you honor your authentic self, celebrate the life you built that brought you to this point, and help you convey to the world through style and organization that, You Have Arrived!

YOU HAVE ARRIVED!

by Lisa Malone

When I sat down to write this chapter, I didn't know where to start because I had so much to share. I love helping others, and service is my love language, but I also don't think anything I do is a big ol' proprietary secret. With this chapter, my goal is to be simple and concise because the hardest part in being an entrepreneur is getting started. It seems easier said than done, but trust me and try by taking one step at a time.

ABOUT ME:

Everyone is on a path, whether they recognize it or not. Decisions you make every day are directing you. So many people are not happy with their path, but don't make changes because they dread change more than their unhappy path. I've changed my path several times in my career, and I'm here to assure you that it isn't as hard or scary as one would think.

I graduated from The Ohio State University (OSU) after a five-year attempt that included two quarters of community college when my father pulled me out of OSU so I could "redistribute my priorities." I stumbled into my third major change to get a Bachelor of Arts degree in Public Relations in the School of Journalism because when I returned to OSU after my "priority redistribution", OSU mistakenly had me categorized as a freshman. I was shut out of all my major courses in advertising. The administration's advice to fix the problem was for me to go door-to-door to request admittance into the classes I needed. So I did.

It didn't occur to me to go back to my list of advertising classes and start there. I had changed my major from a Bachelor of Science degree in business (math and I are not friends) to advertising because advertising seemed easy, no offense to my friends with advertising degrees. Instead, I decided to ask my friends to tell me about the classes they were taking, which ones they loved, and why they loved them. That's when I heard about a fabulous professor and his course which was an introduction to public relations. He took me in and the rest is history!

Fast forward through my 30-year career. My starting job was an outdoor events planner, evolving to a non-profit fund raiser. I soon realized that I needed to reinvent myself as an internet marketing consultant to secure a career change so I could join the dot.com boom. From there, I stumbled into a chance meeting about a perfectly fit position at Microsoft where I evolved from a marketing manager to a channel manager whose responsibility was to grow the Microsoft practice within a technology business who installed Microsoft software. To put it simply, I became a business coach.

The biggest common denominator in most of my life is, when posed with challenge or a hurdle, I took it as a sign to try something different. Someone recently described me as an adrenaline junkie, but I don't think that is the case. What drives me is meeting new people, learning new things, and finding opportunities to have fun at work. I have an aptitude for project management. I thrive when a task has a specific beginning, middle, and end. I like to see the immediate effects of the fruits of my labor because it fuels me to keep going. I know what I am good at and have a lot more success fine tuning my strengths than trying to fix my weaknesses.

SUCCESS STORY:

My reinvention from corporate software sales and channel management to professional organizer came by accident (see aforementioned point about receiving signs to try something different). I quit my corporate software sales job with the plan to take over a small business my husband started that was complementary to my Microsoft experience. Then Covid hit. Without travel to conferences and events, which was the fun part of running his small business, I quickly completed all the boring tasks and became bored silly. I started organizing people's homes to avoid going insane.

I started with family and friends because I didn't know if I'd be good at it and figured no one could complain as I tried new techniques and products. It turned out that organizing is a particular sweet spot for me. It is also a form of self-care, even if it wasn't my home I was organizing, and I was feeding my love language of service. I honestly was doing it for me and my happiness, more than I was doing it for others.

The response was so positive, I put up a website, started posting free tips in my neighborhood Facebook Groups, and quickly developed a client base. The part of the job that continues to feed my soul and confirms I am on the right path is that I have seen couples and families go from feeling resentful towards each other to working together as a team. They started to speak lovingly about each other, simply from getting rid of clutter and creating systems to keep their home organized. Turning chaos to calm is a popular tagline for professional organizers because it is true. The emotional and physical stress of clutter and disorganization takes a huge toll on relationships and families.

Every client I have worked with is brilliant in their career and has created a loving home for their family. Where they struggle is taking the time to make life easy for themselves. They find it hard to take a moment to breathe and enjoy the fruits of their labor. They are too busy working. Society's mantra is work hard, play hard, and be everything for everyone. It's hard to constantly fight that societal pressure.

My clients' either put their children first, giving up 90% of their space to kids' toys because they are over correcting, or they hang on to a past or future self. That means their homes are full of stuff from an old hobby or a future self they hope to be: crafter, gamer, baker, sewer, DIYer, etc. One client described her home as "a house filled with good intentions and zero execution." I get it. But I am here to tell you, **NO ONE** (adult or child) has ever said they missed their "stuff" when it's gone. It's gone because the first step in professional organizing is to **PURGE!** My clients are too busy being thrilled, with the freedom of open spaces and the sense of calm and reenergization their home brings, to miss their "stuff".

MY ADVICE:

My favorite saying is, "when the student is ready, the teacher appears." The fact that you bought this book is a sign that you are open to learning new things. No one person holds the answer for you, but when you are ready for guidance, there are so many influences that will help you uncover what is possible for you on your journey.

From a lifetime of experiences, here are five tips that have never failed me:

1. **Say yes to scary things.** Invitations that make you uncomfortable are hidden doors opening to new possibilities. I suggest saying yes, without thinking... that means:

   - seconds after the invitation is offered
   - the moment before fear talks you out of it

2. **Maximize your strengths** and steer clear of your weaknesses. There's a reason you are better at some things and not so much with others. It's because you were born with an aptitude, or strength, in something—math, science, art, music, etc. If you hate what you are doing and are not good at it, think about how fun and fulfilling life would be if you were doing something you loved. Figure out what you are good at and go deep!

3. **Focus on the positive.** Be fueled by the people who lift you up, remind you of your strengths, and cheer you on. It's a cliché, but it takes practice to let go of all the negativity to

free you to do new things. If you have no one or not enough positive people in your life, I am your person!

4. **Don't overthink things, just start.** It's easy to talk yourself out of anything if you sit around overthinking everything. If you simply start, even if it's for 10 minutes a day, you will gain momentum. Every day, take inventory on what you've accomplished. Focus on what you have done and don't beat yourself up if you think you've fallen short. YOU are your biggest cheerleader. See tip #3. YOU need to be one of your people.

5. **There are no shortcuts, so don't give up.** Building a business is a constant churn of testing and trying new approaches. Those who stick with it the longest are the ones who find success because others give up too soon.

JOIN ME:

To expand my reach as a professional organizer, I partnered with another solopreneur, a personal stylist, to create an online course called, *"You Have Arrived!"* Having arrived is a feeling that comes from within. We believe every person should determine their own definition of success, feel proud of their accomplishments, and be influenced from within, not by society. Having arrived is not a final moment in time, but a motivational confidence that builds as you travel your path.

Our goal is to be a part of your journey as you honor your authentic self, celebrate the life you built that brought you to this point, and help you convey that to the world through style and organization. The *"You Have Arrived!"* digital course is designed to take women step by step through the process of determining their personal style, building a wardrobe that serves them, and setting up a boutique style closet resulting in accessible, organized garments and accessories regardless of the size of their closets.

It is our mission to bring styling and organizing solutions to you so you can focus more on your entrepreneurial goals and less on having a closet full of clothes and nothing to wear. Join us at www.youhavearrived.net. Once you sign up for the course, you will part of a large community of others just like you, who will support you as you travel your path. We cannot wait to see you there!

I dedicate this chapter to the children in my life, those I have personally helped raise, and those around the world whom I have "adopted" in order to improve their life circumstances and give them a better foundation so they, too, can find success in the world on their terms.

A HEAD FOR NUMBERS—A HEART FOR CHILDREN

by Barbara Johnson

One of the most critical tools in an Entrepreneur's Success Kit is a way to know their numbers. When I say "knowing" the numbers, I mean tracking those numbers and understanding their impact. Tracking income from all sources, itemizing expenses as they are incurred, and reviewing those numbers to comprehend how they are affecting the bottom line, the profits and loss statements, and realizing what adjustments can be made throughout the year to lower or improve your tax liabilities.

Whether it's a system in place that allows you to record, track and evaluate your numbers, or hiring a bookkeeper to do it for or with you, the importance of tracking, knowing, and evaluating your numbers is critical to an entrepreneur's success.

HOW I GOT MY START.

I am a veteran. I served ten years active duty in the United States Navy. I worked on P3 aircraft fixing the electronic equipment from changing the box on the plane, to repairing the circuit boards inside the box itself. When I left the service, I had a disability and I was lucky to be treated by heart-centered care providers.

I had four different people helping me from a massage therapist, a chiropractor, an acupuncturist and an energy healer working with me weekly to heal my body and emotions. All the people that helped me were truly concerned regarding the progress of my recovery and about my success in the future. It was by working with such dedicated health and wellness professionals that serving them became my mission, my passion, and my purpose.

For a while, I worked at a game store, and later, at Verizon. While I worked at the game store, I started as an employee and then worked my way up to manager. As manager, they needed someone to help with the bookkeeping and handling inventory and all those tasks that effected the revenue of the store. I would perform both of those functions, but my favorite part was doing the bookkeeping side. So I decided to use my GI Bill to get my accounting degree because I loved it so much.

When I graduated with my accounting degree, I started working for a tax preparation firm, preparing tax returns. And while doing that I got my Enrolled Agent's license. What I found was that a lot of people in business would just throw their receipts into an envelope or a box, and never look at them. They would bring in their box at tax time, not really knowing what they had. They did **NOT** know their numbers! Most of them didn't want to take time from helping clients to deal with the receipts. They knew they needed them. Just didn't want to do anything other than keep them. It took too much time from what they really wanted to do—help people.

I discovered I really enjoy making sense out of other peoples' chaos. For me, it's like putting together a big financial puzzle. While it's actually solving the logic puzzle, I also appreciate the proverbial "beautiful picture" we have when that puzzle is completed! And that also means a better financial recordkeeping and financial outcome for their businesses!

WHAT MAKES MY BUSINESS UNIQUE AND WHY THAT MATTERS.

First and foremost, I am a heart-centered accountant— something you don't see very often at all—almost non-existent. This makes me very unique in my field. Heart-centered is not just who I am, but also who I serve. I love to help people who want to make the world a better place by helping other people. This shared approach to business is what allows me to create such strong working relationships with my clients.

My **WHY** is not to simply make money, but rather it's to help support, and advocate for children and animals around the world. I donate a portion of my profits to organizations such as ChildFund, as well as having a personal vision to provide full-time support of missionaries in their work. And I am also helping with the creation of two animal sanctuaries.

I know the purpose and passion behind my accounting business is unique and a much different approach than most other accountants and bookkeepers you will find. I feel called to make the world a better place by contributing in such ways that will improve or eradicate injustices I have witnessed. And I always find a strong connection with other entrepreneurs who have a powerful passion or purpose behind their own businesses.

You cannot manage or improve what you do not know/track! Knowing your numbers and periodically evaluating them prompts you to make timely adjustments which will make you more successful. If you don't know your numbers, or don't track your expenses, and don't review the data on a regular basis, this will be detrimental in the long run because you are probably missing a lot of areas that are **COSTING** you money.

If you just collect receipts in an envelope or the proverbial "shoebox", and don't look at it until tax time early the following year, you're not able to strategize about what can be done to help you keep more of what you work so hard to earn! From cutting back or increasing expenditures to catching errors in your records, not waiting until year end will put you in a better position come tax time.

Monthly insight into your numbers allows you to adjust your strategy to buy a new computer to offset extra income, or not bill that client until next year in order to reduce your current year income. There are many strategies that can work to your benefit in saving money, if you work with someone and keep track of your numbers monthly.

FIVE ACTION STEPS TO GROW YOUR BUSINESS

1. **Track your income based on category** or type of income, such as affiliate income; sale of product; sale of coaching services; etc. This can lead to success because you can determine where to focus. If one area is increasing and another area declining, it will show you that you should place greater emphasis on the area that is growing.

2. **Be sure that you are tracking and itemizing expenses** such as mileage; office supplies; coaching for your self-development; home office expenses; marketing; networking; etc. Itemizing these expenses can help offset income because most are tax deductible if they comply with certain parameters – and I can help you assess this for your business!

3. **Have a business bank account** that is totally separate from your personal account(s), and do **NOT** under any circumstances ever mix the two. Keeping these finances completely separate is the best way to know your numbers and stay in compliance with Internal Revenue Service (IRS) constraints.

4. **Consult with your accountant** on the best business entity for your particular circumstances. There are benefits to being an S Corporation, forming a Limited Liability Company (LLC), Sole Proprietorship, C Corporation, and Partnership. Your Accountant knows the benefits and requirements of each entity and can evaluate the specific nuances of your business and make appropriate recommendations that will be best for you and your business.

5. **Hire a professional who stays in compliance** with their certifications and up to date with the new regulations the IRS releases quite frequently. The amount you spend for these professional services will likely save you that much and often more in the long run for things they know that you, as an amateur would never know. Plus, you don't have to waste your time trying to focus on things you may not enjoy, allowing you to focus on the areas of your business and things that you enjoy, knowing that your books and finances are in the hands of an expert. It's a win/win!

ONE MORE THING.

Most people aren't crazy about doing their books (and I love doing books, making order out of chaos), and solving the puzzle! Knowing your books is **ESSENTIAL** if you want to:

- Stay in business
- See it grow
- Keep more of what you earn
- Ensure that you give the IRS only what they are owed and no more

The big question for you: Is bookkeeping the highest and best use of **YOUR** time?

YOU DON'T HAVE TO DO IT YOURSELF!

Contact me now and let me show you how having your books done for you is less costly than you think and can give you back more time than you can imagine. And by working with me, you will be giving back to some amazing causes!

Barbara Johnson, *The Heart-Centered Accountant*

barbara.johnson@kisbaa.com | 321.320.2560 (text)

Link to my Evergreen Product:
https://4qm5qmm0.pages.infusionsoft.net/?affiliate=0

I dedicate my chapter to the ones who are full of love but have no voice and yet, are our greatest teachers.... the animals.

PREPARING FOR THE UNEXPECTED (EMERGENCY)

by Kate Klasen

I grew up in a first responder household, specifically, in a fire-house. My dad, grandfather, and uncles were all firemen. When I was old enough to be accepted, I became an EMT. I thought that was what I wanted to do, but life had another idea for me. I went on to become a vet tech. I did that for a few years and enjoyed that job but life again had another plan for me. That is when I got a job as a 9-1-1 dispatcher. I was a dispatcher for eight years and during those years I was a field training officer in the communications department. I eventually became bored with that work and went to the other side of the radio and finished my career as a police officer. I was the only law enforcement in the family, but I kept ties with my EMT side by teaching CPR/First Aid to first responders. I taught at the local police academy, was responsible for teaching my department, and assisted other departments. I taught CPR/First Aid and was also a taser instructor. After almost 20 years, I left law enforcement to move closer to family.

I went back into the pet profession world because I experienced a lot of trauma in my work as an EMT and police officer and needed to move away from working with people. I knew on an emotional level; it was time to heal. I was hired at a veterinary office and worked as a vet assistant while I worked with a groomer to learn the skills of grooming.

During this transition time, my five-pound chihuahua choked one morning after feeding her breakfast. I picked her up and my first thought was, How do you do the Heimlich on a 5lb dog? Oddly, this was not something as a vet tech or vet assistant I was taught (because we are in the hospital setting). My body and my mind weren't in sync, but luckily my body reacted enough and whatever it did, it dislodged the object. I don't know exactly what I did, but it worked. When things settled down, the realization hit that I had almost just lost my dog. The feeling of helplessness was not something, as a former first responder, that sat well with me. I knew at that moment that I needed to learn CPR/first aid for my pets.

I took a class to learn these skills and instantly knew I had to teach it as well! I became an instructor, and now my goal is to teach these skills as much as I can. I have found that many people don't know it's a real thing or they think it's funny. In the pet profession world, it is **NOT** a requirement to learn CPR/first aid and yet they have many animals in their care on a daily basis. My goal is to teach people, not only the techniques but to educate people on the seriousness of this work. I have since saved my chihuahua twice, the second time she choked and I had to perform CPR to bring her back. Another instance, I had a client's dog pass away on my grooming table and I was able to bring the dog back after doing CPR.

The helpless feeling no longer resides in my heart, but I don't ever want anyone who has a pet or cares for pets to have to feel the way I did in that moment. I want a bigger network for our pets, since our pets only have us to be their emergency network. There is no 9-1-1 for our pets. We are their first responders. The more people are trained, the more successful outcomes our pets will have.

My business is unique because it is a niche that most aren't aware of. We are now in a day and age where our pets are not just our family, but travel with us as well. When I am out and about, I like to observe the things most people don't pay attention to. I see pets at restaurants, at stores, at fairs, and many more places. We want them with us! We enjoy their company and all the love they share. We are in more and more areas where pets are welcomed and are now part of situations they weren't really included in, in the past. Growing up, I never saw pets in the areas I see today. This is why emergency training is so important to know.

Would you know what to do if you were at a restaurant patio enjoying your dinner when another patrons dog started choking on something that fell onto the ground?

Would you know what to do if you were at a fair with your pet enjoying the outdoor festivities and another dog passed by that decided it was going to start a fight?

What about traveling with your pet? Do you know how to properly secure the animal in case an accident were to happen?

I see so many pets riding unsecured, or even on the driver's lap. We forget the impact when an accident occurs, and how an air bag could be unsafe for an unsecured pet. We include them in our daily activities and yet don't think about the things that we might encounter.

I have discovered, through talking with people and listening to comments that have been said to me, the thought process is "I'll take them to the vet." I understand that thought, I really do. But, if that was the best answer, "take them to the doctor," then why do we have such an advanced emergency network for ourselves vs. just driving to the doctor? Because time is not on our side when these situations happen. Yes, you will end up at the veterinary office, but the time it takes to get there and what you do is the most important factor for a chance at a successful outcome.

IMPACT: I have had personal successful stories after performing CPR/first aid, but I also have had students who have contacted me after taking the class. I have gotten thank you's from them because during emergency stories that no one ever expected to happen, they were trained, they knew what to do. While not all have been a happy ending, they knew they did everything they could in that moment, and that is priceless.

My business journey has been a learning journey. I didn't grow up in a family that owned or operated businesses, they were first responders or office employees. In school, I never took business classes, I liked biology and science. I had no examples of business ownership. When I was leaving my career in law enforcement, I had no clue what I was going to do. I sat with my neighbor one night with a cup of coffee and discussed what I liked to do. I said "I love animals and they have always been a huge part of my life." That's when I contacted my mobile groomer at the time and asked if I could do a ride along so I could get an idea of what the job entails, and that started my grooming path. I knew in my heart I had to jump and make the move. I couldn't explain it, I just knew I had to go. At 42, I left my career, moved out of state, and went on the adventure to start all over again and re-invent myself. It wasn't easy and I had no clue what I was doing.

I learned from the groomer I was training with, some aspects of business. I also sought out my local **SCORE** chapter and set up consultations with their mentors. I talked with other business owners, all the while I was still learning the skill to create a business. I worked at a veterinary office as front desk and an assistant on the days I wasn't working with the groomer and learning those skills. I was supposed to get hired by the groomer I was working with when I was ready, but she had decided to go another way. I was stumped, what now? I was lucky enough to have the opportunity to rent a room in the vet office and started my grooming business inside the vet office I was working in. I gained a client base, and after a couple years ventured out on my own to open my own salon. I stayed local and almost all my clients followed me. I was able to open my doors with a steady stream of customers. Seven years later, I am still grooming dogs that I started with.

What I never did was start with a business plan and pondered why it was a bad idea. I just moved forward to the next step and it would always work out. I have been very lucky that way, and maybe it has been successful because I don't go negative. I do vision boards and set a goal and go for it. I have definitely learned the universe provides when you are in sync with your path, you put the work in, and do it from the heart. I have always, and still to this day, acknowledge I do what I do because I want to give back to the animal community since they have always been by my side.

I continue on my journey since my body has communicated it doesn't want to groom anymore. Now at 49, I am restructuring once again to teach. In my first year, I have already become a public speaker, done online seminars, been on podcasts, been featured in pet magazines and more. Things that are very out of my comfort zone! My goal is to build this business into an emergency training center for people and pets. I want to build the knowledge and confidence for people to have successful outcomes when time is not on our side.

ACTION STEPS

1. ### Follow Your Intuition

   When I figured out I had burnt out on my law enforcement career, I had to carefully evaluate my next steps. If, like me, you have a certain skill set and a passion you can easily combine—like CPR and pets—then voila! You have the formula to build your own business and create a life and career you love.

2. ### Always Focus on Your Success or Belief Matters

   Your entrepreneurial journey will have its ups and downs. By creating your future vision and going for it with an unstoppable level of passion and commitment (and hard work) will help you succeed. There will be days you want to quit, but don't give up!

3. Seek Out Mentors

The best way to fast track your success is to seek out others doing what you want to do—whether they do what you do and are financially successful or you see their social media is on point—do not hesitate to set up a call or meeting to ask them how they got there. Learning from successful people's wins (and lessons learned from losses) will help you skip over the road bumps and level up faster. There are local groups out there that want to really help you with your journey, search them out and utilize what is available to you.

4. Be Flexible

Just like I re-imagined my business at 49, you must always allow yourself the grace and space to change things up. Life happens and without some flexibility in your business plans, you will have a hard time evolving to meet the current market and staying competitive. Listen to your gut, it will always guide you in the right direction.

5. Know You are Making a Difference

When in doubt, reach out to those clients you have truly helped. Not only to keep yourself motivated, but also to capture invaluable testimonials to help promote your business to others who need what you have to offer. You started your business for a reason, so keep going and know you are changing lives one client at a time!

"Once you replace your negative thoughts with positive ones, you'll start having positive experiences" - Laura Enzor

EVICTING NEGATIVE NELLIE FROM YOUR HEADSPACE

by Laura Enzor

I never planned on becoming a life coach. I was always the creative type. I majored in modern dance performance and later morphed that talent into becoming a fitness pro. Fast forward to add Lyme disease-butt-kicker and Reinvention Coach for women to my titles.

I came into my own in the fitness world. I found my voice, and was living with purpose and passion. But if I were to be honest, Negative Nellie was a big part of my life even then. Nellie did her best to keep me on the "straight and narrow." She helped me be hard on myself, constantly watching the scale. I pushed myself to participate in a women's physique contest and walked away with the first-place trophy. I learned that if I put my heart, soul, and time into something, I could accomplish whatever I set out to do. I admit that my perfectionistic tendencies helped me make some outstanding gains in fitness which set me apart from the rest of the pack.

But it came with a price.

There was a lot of inner talk about carbs being the enemy, making sure I only ate chicken, broccoli, and sweet potatoes every day along with eight scrambled egg whites and my after training, protein smoothie. If I slipped from that strict diet, I would curse at myself.

"Why did you eat that? Three pieces of pizza, really? It's going to take all week to burn that off."

If I gained more than five pounds, I wouldn't show up to the gym until I lost the weight. I have never told anyone that and it's painful to admit. I thought that if no one heard my negative inner chatter, everything was good. While in my 20's and 30's, I devoted my time and energy to my fitness regimen. I enjoyed my work, and loved being in the spotlight, but I didn't love myself. I never seemed to accept myself when I was, "less than perfect." Perfect began to become a problem, but I held on tight because it brought me a lot of achievements...

until it didn't.

Life, as it will, threw me a curve ball. My body was starting to fail me. I began experiencing joint pain, fatigue, moodiness. I was turning 40, and I started to run out of motivation at the gym. I was frustrated with myself and not happy with losing muscle mass. I would proceed to "push" through life for the next ten years, traveling and moving all over the world due to my husband's job. On the one hand, I was having the time of my life, but I was still ignoring the signals my body was sending me. When I finally dragged myself into the Doctor's office, they blamed everything on hormones and the fact that I was moving every two to three years.

"Go home and rest," was the doctor's advice.

I was dismissed by many doctors because, from the outside, I looked like the picture of health.

I managed to make a comeback with my health and with my career when we moved back from an overseas stint in Luxembourg. I found a doctor who gave me thyroid medicine and within two years, my health stabilized and I landed my dream job in fitness. At the same time, my husband decided he wanted to try something new which would mean moving us to Arizona.

"No, I don't want to move, I just finally got my health back and I'm ready to step into the new job I have spent months training for."

But I caved in for the umpteenth time.

"This is what you're supposed to do as a wife and mother. It's too late to change my life anyway, so just go with the flow," I said quietly to myself.

I prided myself on being easy-going, not making waves, striving to be the model mother, the perfect wife, the ambitious fitness professional, and the fun friend. I set aside my own, big picture, dreams time and time again, subjugating my needs to fit around the edges of everyone else around me. There was no time for me to follow through on anything beyond teaching my fitness classes, training clients in my basement, and whipping up dinner every night. I wanted to do more, create more, and be more of a fitness personality, but life was busy. I just kept thinking after the next move, after my daughter was in middle school, after my husband gets the next job opportunity, then I would be able to tap back into my creative core.

So, I was patient, but the years kept ticking by.

Soon after the move to Arizona, I was diagnosed with Lyme disease. It had already progressed and been doing damage for ten years. Can you imagine the voice of negativity?

"Why me? I'm the healthiest person I know, this isn't fair, no one wants to hang out with a sick person. I can't go on those hikes I used to enjoy so much, my life sucks, I have nothing to offer anymore."

Negative Nellie's voice grew louder as I lost, faith, hope, and a vision for my future. I had disregarded all the physical symptoms and pushed through like a champ, wore the super woman cape like it was a badge of honor, and ended up with a chronic illness. Negative Nellie would point out all the things I was missing out on, how I was only getting older, telling me if I waited any longer I was going to be all washed up. And worse things were said like, it's over for you, you lost your one opportunity, loser, things never work out for you, it's not about what you want, so get over it."

LETTING NELLIE GO

I have lived with my Negative Nellie for a long time, so, perhaps I can spare you the crash and burn part. Because Negative Nellie is all about the crash and burn cycle.

I'm hoping you are starting to see that negativity can bring you down from the inside unless you start to acknowledge it and bring the negative thoughts into the light. I want to share with you five ways that you can start calling out your negative self-talk and start to shift some of those negative patterns. Your health and happiness depends on it!!

FIVE WAYS TO EVICT NEGATIVE NELLIE FROM YOUR HEADSPACE:

1. **ACKNOWLEDGE YOUR NEGATIVE SELF-TALK.** What are the words you're saying to yourself, either quietly or out loud? Look at the ways you criticize yourself, your life or other people. For a solid 5 days, record all your negative self-talk, keep a notepad or use your phone. Call the negative thoughts out! Get really, honest with yourself. This is a critical first step!

2. **GIVE YOUR NEGATIVE SELF- TALK A NAME.** Negative Nellie, Naysaying Nancy, Knucklehead Nissa, whatever you would like. Get creative! You internalized this negative voice based on your past experiences. Separate it from your authentic self because it is NOT part of the real you.

3. **ASK YOURSELF, IS THIS TRUE?** Are you really, stupid, not good enough for prime time, or a horrible public speaker? Comb through your life and look for evidence that refutes those nasty claims. Take it in and see the real truth.

4. **CREATE NEW EMPOWERING AFFIRMATIONS** to replace the negative self-talk you've become accustomed to. Make them actionable, inspiring, and reasonable.

Take from the example above. "I am a horrible public speaker." And change it to, "I am becoming a magnetic speaker" or "I am a magnetic speaker and people want to hear what I have to say." It might feel a bit uncomfortable but that's when you know you're on the right track!

5. **TAKE THE ONE AFFIRMATION THAT YOU NEED MOST** right now and write it on several sticky notes. Place one on your bathroom mirror, refrigerator, computer or desk, all the places where you will see it daily and repeat it.

Come up with a plan. Consider things like... when I take my walk I will say it over and over for at least five minutes (it's best when you are distracting yourself with movement and opening up your subconscious mind. It will have no choice but to listen in and replace the negative thoughts with the new positive, and empowering thoughts.) You can even set a timer on your phone to stop and say it out loud. Stick with it for a month remembering how many times you proved the lie to be false.

Your negative thoughts were developed when you were younger based off of a shadow belief that you created about yourself sometime under the age of ten. A dramatic event likely happened, and because you were too young to discern what was going on, you made it mean something about you. Then this belief got stored in your operating system in your subconscious mind only to show up right when you're about to push your personal edge or are faced with an unanticipated turn of events. It's what we call, in coaching, your auto-pilot response. It's pre-programmed. The negative thoughts are an automatic response. So, depending on the severity of these dramatic situations, you may be able to flip the script on your negative self-talk by going through the five- steps above. At the end of this chapter, I've provided a link to a more in depth-worksheet to guide you through this process.

But for deeply ingrained beliefs, I recommend working with a life coach, trained in releasing shadow beliefs. Since the shadow beliefs are the source from which your negative thoughts arise- uncovering, reframing, and transforming your beliefs will allow you to evict Negative Nellie from your headspace for good. Working with a coach can help fast track you to living your best life, the kind of life that you'll love to wake up to every morning!

From the outside looking in, you may have built a comfortable life for yourself and your family, maybe even a life most envy. But if you have that ache in your heart that tells you something is missing, then consider a coach. It doesn't have to be me, but I strongly advise coaching as it HAS changed my life for the better. I went from hopeless to hopeful and thriving, even WITH a chronic illness!!!

MY EXPERIENCE WORKING WITH A COACH

With a willingness to take soul-aligned action and make decisions with MY dreams at the forefront, I decided to dig deep, and hire someone to help me. Boy that was tough. I am not the type to ask for help. Also, I sought out life coaching because, quite frankly, therapy wasn't what I needed. I wanted to move out of the crappy mindset I was in and move out fast! I needed a more action-oriented program. With focus and commitment, I found my magic, unraveled the beliefs that were holding me hostage, and reconnected with my creative core.

Your creative core is the blueprint for living a soul-satisfying life and it's at the heart of the Reinvention Coaching process. I gained the courage to have a serious "talking to" with Nellie. She learned that I was in charge, and she had no choice but to back off, go to her corner, and stop running the show. I then got hooked on transformation and got certified, not once but twice! And I am still adding onto my certifications. Now I'm a reinvention coach for women and I know for certain that negative self-talk can have a devastating impact on your ability to get what you want in life, feel good about yourself, and really thrive. After all we are what we think.

When you change a belief you change your life, it's that powerful.

Maybe YOU'VE been putting off realizing your dreams or taking your business to the next level? You're too old, too young, not pretty enough, not tall enough, not a good public speaker etc. etc.

When you're not in alignment with what you say you want—whether we're talking about your ideal family life, how you want to feel about yourself, or the aspirations you have for your business, the negative thoughts in one area will bleed over into the other. If even one of those area's is out of alignment, it can cause dis-ease and disruption in your life and prevent you from enjoying your journey.

I am passionate about creatively empowering women to connect with their wholeness and worthiness, so they can manifest their highest positive vibrations and live a life on fire.

Don't you want to feel peace, positivity, and fulfillment in the work you do and in the way you live your life? I hope so. I certainly want that for you!

Below is the free worksheet "Calling out Negative Nellie"

https://www.lauraenzor.com/calling-out-negative-nellie

Here's a link to book a free coaching call if you're interested in taking a deeper dive

https://www.lauraenzor.com/schedule-free-coaching-call

I also help women through my mind, body spirit workshop called *AffirMotion* which I offer in the Scottsdale and Sedona areas in Arizona. *AffirMotion* is an extension of my mission to help raise up the positive vibe of the female collective by creating an experience for women to connect, deepen, imprint, and manifest their own highest positive vibrations by merging the magic of affirmations with the power of movement. I leverage my skills as a choreographer and life coach to bring forth this creative workshop.

I believe every woman has the potential to transform their life if given the right tools.

Cliche as it is-Dedicating this chapter to Zafar, my husband who literally is my knight in shining armor and my four kids (Zacharia, Zara, Zayd, Zan) who are the constant blessings in my life.

ACHIEVING WORK LIFE ALIGNMENT

by Zaiba Hasan

I'm Zaiba Hasan, a corporate wellness specialist and spiritual parenting coach who specializes in working with women of color, particularly mothers, who are often in the corporate world. I'm also a woman of color myself. Mom is of Irish descent and Dad is from Pakistan making me biracial, multi-world, and multi-cultural. I have my Master's Degree in divinity and I am able to connect with different religions which allows me to come from a spiritual place in my coaching.

I am the mother of four amazing kids, three of whom are boys, who I am raising to be good citizens. I make the joke that God sent me boys to raise because I have never been very fond of men. This is my chance to teach my boys to be the kind of men the world needs more of. As a certified spiritual parenting coach, I work with people from many religions. I have learned that from a parenting aspect, we all want what is best for our children. This is where we all meet regardless of our faith or beliefs.

MY PERSONAL JOURNEY:

I came to a realization during the pandemic that my coaching was falling hallow. I was coaching women to be their best selves but I was not following my own advice. This began to directly impact my health, both physical and spiritual.

I contracted Covid-19 early on and was sick for nearly a year. In fact, despite being vaccinated and having all the booster shots, I got Covid two more times. Being sick made work difficult as well as parenting my own children. My doctors were concerned as to why I was so susceptible to the disease and ran a battery of tests including a hospital-sponsored study. I was not recovering, and through the testing, my doctor found that I had far more than Covid. I had a slew of other issues including fatty liver, thyroid, hormone imbalances, and auto immune issues. In short, I was a bit of a mess.

I found myself using food to cope with my emotions and childhood trauma. I was creating the persona of a super busy, serial entrepreneur and super mom. I was doing all that I could to avoid the underlying issues I had. By helping others, I recognized that I was not doing the work for myself.

I began to do the hard work. I started intense therapy including EMDR which I attribute to saving my life. I knew I had to combat the intergenerational trauma so, as a mother, I would not pass this along to my children. I began cutting people out of my life, including family members. It was hard but necessary for my healing.

I focused on recognizing that food was poisoning my body. In dealing with my stress triggers, I was using food to cope with those trigger points during the day. The EMDR therapy, while life changing, exposes those triggers and physical responses while offering tools and techniques to cope with the issues that are brought to light. But for a few days after each session, those traumas are front and center and triggers abound.

I kept myself busy and ate pretty healthy during the day—salads mostly—or I skipped meals. As the day wore on, by evening I would start to use food, especially sugar and caffeine, to work through the emotions that were welling up from therapy. The doctors had found tumors on my thyroid and this added to my steady weight gain. I wasn't sleeping well either which was screwing up my hormones.

Here I was coaching people and working to help people, particularly women like myself, live a healthy life while I was not. I had to come to terms with that fact and face it. Mind you, I don't smoke or drink. I am of Muslim decent and my spiritual background keeps me from those unhealthy acts. But there was still the matter of food.

We women say that we would die for our children, but my question is, are we actually living for them? We need to be living our best life so we can model that for our kids. I had gained a great deal of weight over a four-year period while exposing all my trauma. Once I began to realize that I was not eating for fuel but rather I was eating my emotions, I was able to make real changes. I had to cure the trauma that was manifesting itself in so many ways. My daughter coming of age, triggered something in me that made me want to effect real change. I was telling myself that I was doing amazingly well, homeschooling kids, succeeding in my work, but I was not being truthful.

I went on a quest to change my life. I began with a two month fast to regulate my hormones. I talked about spiritual cleansing in my work and even though I had gained a great deal of weight, was dealing with stress, poor health, and trauma, I was still able to help other people with their health journey. I believe my appeal was my honesty about my own struggles. I was able to express that we were in this together.

As a mother, I put everyone else first, however, I was preaching the exact opposite in my coaching. I had been literally killing myself. Slowly, as I did the work, I lost the 100 pounds I had gained and kept it off. I was always athletic and healthy and knew that I could get back to that version of myself. I went on a spiritual cleanse as well and continued to study brain science.

Today, I wake up every morning at 4:30AM. I start my day with meditation, yoga, and strength training. One niche of mine is that I am a Hormonal Sleep Specialist and I am one of the very few certified in that field in the US. This is important for women specifically as sleep issues are the number one thing that women are dealing with and don't understand.

As a parenting coach, I focus on the parents more than the children. I work to build a strong foundation with both parents though more so mothers because in the Western world, we have created a system where women are not getting the support they need, especially mothers.

I believe that women need to support each other in much better and deeper ways. We are often our own worst enemies and not as supportive as we can be to one another or even to ourselves. With my program, I am creating that sort of support system. I am not about normalizing the need to wear make-up, dress a certain way, or act a certain way to please societal norms. I am more about being authentic.

My mission is to create a platform which includes my podcast called *Mommying While Muslim* that showcases women within our community. It's a no man zone where guests are concerned – the mic on my show goes to women who can do anything their male counterparts can.

My platform is for women to always feel supported and to give them the tangible tools to make the change within themselves. We are all empowered to make the changes we need to make. My job is to get you there with the tools I have developed.

FIVE TIPS FOR WOMEN ENTREPRENEURS:

1. **Dismiss the notion of Work Life Balance.**

   There is no such thing. Women are constantly trying to pursue this idea and it will inevitably fail. I prefer to rename this to Work Life Alignment. Some things in life take priority over others. Be okay with that. Ex: If I am working on a big project, my house might be mess. I might not be coming home early enough to cook and may have to Door Dash dinner. Some stuff goes to the wayside.

   If you feel like you have to create total balance like the libra scale, you are putting too much pressure on yourself. Let it go. You can have a bad day. Let yourself have a healing day when needed, feel your emotions. That can be a very productive day. Many women feel like they are a failure if everything isn't perfect. It's my job to say, its ok to not take a shower, stay in your jammies, and focus on a project. You can teach the kids to do the cooking, you can hire people to clean, you don't have to be perfect. Stop believing the hype of social media. Do what is normal for you, what aligns with your best life on your terms.

2. **Putting up boundaries, even with work, family, and friends.**

    Tele-work has made that harder. It's hard to grasp but you can say no to things. We all think if we say no to an opportunity it's the last opportunity we are going to have, but what is the point if that opportunity is negatively impacting your health and your life? And will that opportunity help you on your spiritual or life journey? As you get more success under your belt, you will begin to realize that you can let the wrong opportunities go. Better ones will come because you made the room for them.

3. **Don't try to coach or train others on something you yourself can't or won't do.**

    Think about your **WHY**. What is your actual superpower? What do you want to offer to the world? Figure that out and work on that. Offer that to others. Don't pretend to be someone you are not. Be authentic.

4. **Self-care can be simple.**

    Stop trying to over complicate it. It's great to go to the spa, get a massage, get your hair and nails done, but self-care can be just five minutes you give to yourself here and there during the day. It can be a walk with the dog or sitting with a cup of tea on your back porch. Just be present. Sometimes I just sit, no TV, no phone, no listening to podcasts. When you are present you experience things you might otherwise miss. I love to sit outside early in the morning. As the sun comes up, the birds sing so loudly and so beautifully. Pick things that nourish you even if for a few minutes a few times a day.

5. Allow yourself permission to do **NOTHING.**

In our crazy busy worlds, we take pride in being busy however true healing allows for rest. In creating mandatory breaks within your day you create opportunities for efficiency. If we are fatigued, we will not be our best selves.

If what I have said resonates with you, I would like to invite you to join our Facebook Community to keep updated on all of our amazing virtual offerings.

Emerge Consulting Solutions | McLean VA | Facebook

> *You deserve the life you crave. I'll support you getting there.*

MY JOURNEY FROM SELF-DOUBT TO ENTREPRENEURSHIP

by Jennifer McClain

I am Jennifer McClain, and I am a social impact leader and Certified Life and Leadership Coach who is passionate about helping women build the confidence to invest in themselves and their growth. This is a far cry from my childhood dream of becoming an attorney (anyone else a big fan of Claire Huxtable on The Cosby Show?) until my reality check as an introvert and my love for math and science redirected me into computer science as my major in college. Still, after receiving my BS in Computer Science, fate found me struggling to find a tech job and "falling" into non-profit work and here I am, today, following my calling serving under-resourced communities and individuals striving to increase their wages and grow their assets.

While working at the Abraham Lincoln Centre, a community support and resource non-profit in Chicago, I experienced my first professional coaching/mentoring when discussing potential job opportunities. My supervisor, the COO, challenged me to not just seek a higher paycheck, but asked me to figure out what I loved to do. He insisted if I had that answer, the money etc. would fall in place. It took me a while to figure that out, so I focused on developing and growing by receiving an MBA and a Master's in Public Administration—with a concentration in nonprofit management. After being promoted to Director at my current employer (Local Initiatives Support Corporation) I participated in my first leadership development program. There I had the opportunity to engage with an Executive Coach to help me push myself further by focusing on the impact that I wanted to have and developing my leadership abilities. I also attended train the trainer sessions...I was on the personal growth and development track and never looking back!

My desire to launch *Mission ENSPIRE* grew from this coaching and training I've been fortunate to receive during my career in the nonprofit sector. These resources have been foundational to my success as a leader in the nonprofit and faith communities. For more than 20 years, I have managed teams and bolstered community-centered nonprofits, while providing community leadership as a board member and faith leader. Since 2013, as an expert facilitator, I have led sessions attended by more than 800 participants in areas including, but not limited to, financial, career, supervisory, and leadership coaching.

I credit my coaching expertise and training to field leaders such as Central New Mexico Community College (CNMCC), Tribe Coaching, The Prosperity Agenda, NeighborWorks America and Academy of Creative Coaching. I further developed my coaching skills through CNMCC's and The Prosperity Agenda's "train the trainer" sessions and most recently as a Coaching for Everyone Scholar. My success and career trajectory would not have been possible without meaningful coaching, training, and leadership development opportunities. And now I am determined to pay it forward.

I founded my purpose-driven company, *Mission ENSPIRE*, LLC, to provide coaching, training, facilitation, and consulting services to help clients achieve success and fulfillment in their personal and professional lives. My primary audience is women, particularly those in the nonprofit or faith communities. Through *Mission ENSPIRE*, I create space for clients to overcome doubts or insecurities, define their purpose, and operate at their fullest potential.

Like me when I started out, many of my peers—particularly women and people of color—have a strong desire for personal or professional coaching services but struggle to connect to the right resources. This may stem from a lack of awareness or access to services, or the lack confidence to invest time or money into their own self-improvement. This last barrier is acute among many people who work in the nonprofit sector or in faith institutions, and who prioritize service to others. They may, at times, place their own needs on the back burner. I created *Mission ENSPIRE* to fill this gap, by helping clients to prioritize 'self' and strive for greatness. Through our coaching and training services, *Mission ENSPIRE* will create a global community of women and organizations who Envision New Solutions and Possibilities that Inspire Results and Empowerment (E.N.S.P.I.R.E.).

Mission ENSPIRE was born of an unmet need. We create space for women, nonprofit professionals, and faith leaders to overcome doubts or insecurities, and chart their paths to personal, business, or organizational success. Our client-driven model is rooted in coaching and the belief that every client is the expert of their own life experience, preferences, and goals.

I'm a single mother of two young adult daughters, a woman of faith, a Senior Director at a national nonprofit and I also run my own business. I understand what it means to wear many different hats and not really spend a lot of time on myself. That's the profile of the women that I work with. They wear many hats to support others and tend to not prioritize focusing on themselves. I'm the type of coach that provides personalized support that aids my clients in changing their lives or jobs, becoming "unstuck," or discovering fresh inspiration and direction.

What makes my approach different is also what makes me unique. I approach my coaching with an appreciation for the individual—recognizing differences in how each person learns, works, and communicates. I believe that we are all creative, resourceful, whole and capable and that we have the tools that we need within us but sometimes we don't know it, nor do we know how to tap into it. I never promise to have all the answers, but I definitely ask powerful questions to support my clients in unleashing what is holding them back.

Developing successful business strategies, optimizing success, enhancing quality of life, and navigating transitions in one's job or in one's personal life are just a few of the many personal and professional objectives that as a coach I support my clients with. Active listening is one of my most effective tools as a Coach, which I combine with powerful questions to elicit client-driven strategies and solutions. It's my role as a Certified Life and Leadership Coach to support individuals to achieve the results that are important to their personal journey and success, however they define it.

The positive impact of working with me as a coach is illustrated through Veronica's story:

Veronica was a client who was focusing most of her time with work and her family and not much time on herself. This led to her feeling burnt out, tired, unfulfilled and like she was letting herself down. This created difficulty for her in determining her goals. Like many others, she suffered from an "all or nothing" approach. If Veronica wasn't "all in" on setting and achieving her goals she would do nothing instead which meant that she often failed to execute on the plans that she made for herself.

Veronica realized that she needed assistance coming up with a strategy that would be effective for her and support her in prioritizing the things she wanted to build for herself in her personal life. Despite prior unsuccessful work with other coaches, Veronica started researching coaching programs and came across my "Renew You, Love Your Life Virtual Coaching Program". This was a program that guides you through my 3-step process where you get to the heart of what's holding you back.

Being in the program gave Veronica the opportunity to reflect and figure out what was important to her. She began to prioritize those things, including taking time for herself, which has helped her grow in self-awareness. She felt that the program's framework, questions and assignments provided insight and importantly, accountability.

As a result of taking part in this program, Veronica saw improvement in terms of establishing boundaries, creating time for what she wanted to do, and holding herself accountable. She had more energy, and when she noticed that she was reverting to old behaviors, she went

> back and reviewed the skills she acquired during the program to refocus and redirect herself. She felt that she improved in her capacity to design a life that supports who she wants to be and how she wants to present herself to the world as a result of having received coaching from Jennifer. She applies what she has learned through the coaching in her everyday life.

My entrepreneurial journey as a new business owner who also has a full-time job plus a family hasn't been easy but the following action steps have been pivotal to me getting this far along in my journey.

1. **Find your champions.** Find like-minded people who believe in you, share your vision. People who will provide support and tell you the truth. People you can champion in return. This may come in many forms. I am a member of two professional development groups that have been critical. I am also part of a circle of women colleagues who check in and encourage one another. My family has also been a sounding board. And I couldn't do this without partnering with God in my business by praying about different aspects of my business.

2. **Look for lessons everywhere.** As a proud, life-long learner, I consistently read books and articles, listen to podcasts, and watch Ted Talks to find new ideas and perspectives. I also know that lessons often come in the form of obstacles or mistakes. As a coach, I pride myself on learning alongside my clients – their lessons inform my life and work, creating a virtuous cycle of learning.

3. **Ignore your inner critic.** My inner critic loves to pay the comparison game. She tells me "Look at what so and so is doing, she is so much further ahead than you". I let that voice keep me from starting my business for a very long time, even though I knew it was a part of my purpose and something that I couldn't not do. The way that I push past what the inner critic says is by recognizing that she exists, then remembering who I am, my expertise and the impact that I've made thus far. I use scripture to help remind me what God says about me. I also use affirmations. I also have to remind myself that my journey is mine exclusively; leading me to eliminate comparisons I make with myself and others.

4. **Set. Reflect. Celebrate. Repeat.** We need goals to anchor our vision. But we can't just set goals. We must also take time to reflect on our progress, pivot as needed, and celebrate our achievements. We also have to give ourself grace and not beat ourself up when we don't meet certain goals. Most people are familiar with SMART Goals – specific, measurable, attainable and time-bound. However, I don't believe that most individuals think about the need for a mechanism to assess and acknowledge success once those goals have been stated.

5. **Invest in yourself.** You are worth it! Too many of us, especially women and those in service-oriented careers, struggle to make time or financial commitments necessary to fulfill our personal or professional goals. We hesitate before hiring a coach. We hesitate to enroll in a training. If we don't invest in ourselves, how we can expect others to? The investment has a visible return. I strive to lead my clients by example on this one.

As you have read my story and read these tips ask yourself these questions:

- What are you taking away?
- What is your one action you can implement in the next 30 days?
- How will I hold myself accountable?

If my story resonated with you and you want to learn more about me, connect with me on my website and receive a free gift.

https://missionenspire.com/free-resources/

Let's be self-assured. Let's be decisive. Let's start now and get the life you crave!

I'd like to dedicate this chapter to my mother, Robin Bates, who told me when I was about six years old, that I could grow up to be anything I wanted to be! I truly love that empowering mindset she gave me!

THE SECRET TO ACCESSING YOUR INNER MAGIC

by Melissa Deally

THE WHY...

I was in the corporate world until eight years ago, when suddenly big fish bought little fish, and I was given an hour to clear out my desk. This was after 24 years of service, and with no word of thanks!

In that moment, I knew three things:

- I would never work for anyone else again.

- Whatever I did next had to be more of service to the planet and humanity.

- I had no idea what I would do, but I was open to being guided.

Soon after this I was introduced to a company that specialized in brain supplementation. I found this interesting, as I used my brain 24/7, and yet no one had ever told me that I could do more to look after the health of my brain!

I was intrigued because my own grandmother was 99 years old at the time, fully cognitively functioning, living at home by herself, caring for herself. I was also aware that in Western countries we had near epidemic levels of Alzheimer's / Dementia. I realized if more people could learn how to care for their brain, that would have a huge impact in our world. I also wondered, "I have good genes, but is that enough, for me to get on my grandmother's path and live a long, vibrant life right to the end? (She died in her sleep two weeks past her 101st birthday).

Soon after learning about brain supplementation and developing an interest in learning more about the brain, my oldest daughter sustained a concussion during the first soccer game of her grade 12 year. Two months later, while driving, I received a phone call from the High School, that my younger daughter had sustained a suspected concussion in 8th grade gym class! I literally looked out the windshield at the heavens above and asked "This is how you show me my path? Please, stop taking out my children." So now, I had two very different concussions in our family and was supporting both girls, going to their appointments with them, and using the brain supplements to support their brains' ability to heal.

Throughout this process, I learned that people need more support on their healing journey, and I learned that the body doesn't heal in a stressed-out state. Being guided on your healing journey, allows you to relax into the process, taking you out of the stress state, so you can heal. This is what I was naturally offering my daughters.

I was then invited to work at a local clinic to help others heal from concussions. However, I didn't have any certification, so I couldn't get insurance to work there. This led me to going back to school, and over the next six years, I added Health and Life Coaching, Integrative Health Practitioner, Master Practitioner in NLP, Timeline Therapy and Hypnosis Trainer to my resume.

With all these tools, I've come back to where I started—focusing on the brain—more specifically the power of your unconscious mind, in creating the life, business, and health you want, with guaranteed results! We spend too much time focusing on our conscious mind, which only gives us access to 10% of what is available to us, whereas the unconscious mind gives us access to the other 90 %. If you aren't getting the results you want, it's because you are using the wrong part of your mind!

THE WHAT...

Would you like to learn how to access your inner magic – your unconscious mind? When you work with us you are literally changing your neurology, and then practicing using it, to deepen the neurological pathways so they become ingrained. This is easy to do with NLP, Timeline Therapy, and Hypnotherapy. In fact, here are some stats about Hypnotherapy and how quick and effective it is.

From the US medical association in 1958. A survey of psychotherapy literature by Alfred A. Barrios, PhD, published in American Health magazine, revealed the following:

- **Psychoanalysis:** 38 percent recovery after 600 sessions
- **Behaviour Therapy:** 72 percent recovery after 22 sessions
- **Hypnotherapy:** 93 percent recovery after 6 sessions

When we use the right part of our brain to do the change work, it is quick, effective, and lasting. And here's the thing, all learning, all behaviour, and all change is handled by our unconscious mind, so using conscious methods to create change isn't going to be nearly as effective!

These tools are highly powerful not only in healing, but also in changing behaviours, setting goals, improving your focus, and changing your mindset about certain activities. If for instance, you dislike sales calls, how often do you spend the day procrastinating rather than reaching out to prospective clients? Are you getting the number of clients you need, to achieve your revenue goals? Or perhaps you're good at reaching out the first time, but you dislike follow up, or you only follow up one time? We can re-program your unconscious mind so that you love making sales calls, and love following up, so these required tasks to build a successful business, become enjoyable to you.

When we work with your unconscious mind, we can create big changes with small tweaks. For instance, your values impact your beliefs which impact your behaviours. In NLP, values are the programs that we pick up by living life and having experiences. By changing your values, we automatically shift your beliefs and therefore your behaviour. If you are looking to create a profit in your business, but don't have "money" as one of your key business values, you simply aren't going to be able to generate the kind of money you dream of. The great news is, we can re-program your values held in your unconscious mind to reflect what you want in your business and life!

Do you wish you could achieve more focus in your day-to-day work? Did you know that hypnosis allows for 10,000 times more focus and 50,000 times more accountability? Would this be helpful to you in achieving your business goals? Wouldn't it be great to simply ditch the distractions and just sit down and get it done? With hypnosis, you can! You can learn self-hypnosis and have this tool to use every day, knowing you are working with your unconscious mind to build your business with ease and flow, rather than trying to "do more" and "work harder," as you rely solely on your conscious mind.

Tapping into all these tools, allows you to access the 90% of your brain that is largely ignored by most people. This gives you the competitive advantage, and all you are doing is using what you were born with! The difference is you've been taught how to access this part of your brain, and once you learn this, you have these tools for life. You won't just set smart goals, like everyone else, you'll set quantum smart goals, so you can dream big and turn your dreams into reality.

You'll have the energy to build your business, because you'll have the ability to optimize your health. Your unconscious mind runs all your health programs too – it is charged with keeping you alive, despite what you do! It keeps you breathing, your heart pumping, your digestive system breaks down your food and you don't even give it a moment's notice! Just think what you can do when you start to pay attention and work with your unconscious mind! In hypnosis both parts of the mind, conscious and unconscious work together as one, instead of using just 10% of your brain, you'll have access to 100% of your brain! I love showing people how to access the other 90% of their brain to improve their health, their business results, their life!

THE HOW YOU CAN...

I walk my talk. I don't ask clients to do anything I haven't already done for myself. These five action steps have helped me achieve success and they are the same steps I guide my clients through.

1. Commitment

    Are you ALL in, or just in until it's inconvenient? Commitment requires money, time, and energy have been spent in a legally binding way, without that, there is no business commitment. This law of commitment also applies to the action steps you take in your health, relationships, finances, and spirituality. This action step supersedes all the rest, as they all require commitment too!

2. Prioritize Your Health

    Health is so often ignored and pushed aside when someone is building a business. However, it is critical because building a business is stressful and takes energy and time. When we don't take the time to prioritize our health, we can end up with a myriad of health issues from weight gain, brain fog, low energy, aches & pains to chronic illnesses and burnout. Every single one of these is triggered by stress, in fact 90% of all doctors' appointments are triggered by stress and 65% of all diseases are triggered by stress.

When I learned three steps to set boundaries without conflict, my life changed. Do you know them? (If you don't, that's okay, I cover them in my workshops and trainings.) Boundaries allowed me to create time to look after me! Six in ten North Americans have one chronic illness, four in ten have more than one. The average person is spending the last ten years of their life in a nursing home, at a cost of $108,000 / year and by 2030 that is forecast to be $141,000 / year. Well over $1 million dollars for your nursing home stay. A stay during which your quality of life is greatly diminished, or you simply wouldn't be there.

Is that what you dream of as you build your business? I don't think so! Why are you building your business? Is it for financial freedom, time freedom? Do you dream of travel, and time spent with loved ones? If so, don't give up your health freedom, by ignoring your health as you build your business. Your health truly is your greatest asset, treat it as such. Choose to invest in your health while you invest in your business, by seeking the support of someone who can guide your health journey, so it never becomes an illness journey.

3. Seek Coaching and Mentorship

Do you want to achieve your goals quickly? The fastest way to do this is learn from someone who has already done it before you, instead of wasting time and energy trying to figure out everything for yourself. When you seek the support of a coach or mentor, you will have a recipe to follow and the ability to get your questions answered, so you don't get stuck. You will also have accountability—we tend to give up on ourselves easily, but we don't like to let other people down.

Sometimes we need a re-set on our thoughts—the ones that are telling us, "You can't" or "You aren't good enough," are holding you back. Our thoughts are powerful, they dictate our words, then our actions, which become habits and then beliefs. Are your thoughts getting in the way of your progress? Perhaps it's time to re-program your unconscious mind and release those limiting thoughts and install powerful new thoughts so you can achieve your goals and dreams.

4. Find Your Tribe

As you grow while building your business, you will find that you are outgrowing some people in your life, and that's okay. In life, friends come and go, but notice the ones who are holding you back. They have the best of intentions at heart, they want to keep you safe and from leaving them, so they try to talk you out of your dreams. Don't let them! They are your dreams, not theirs, they don't have the skills and motivation you have, when they say "you can't do it", they are really saying "I can't do it" and projecting that onto you. Don't let this become your belief, protect yourself from it, by finding your tribe and working with your coach/mentor.

5. Personal Growth

I believe we are all put on this earth to do three things:

- Never stop growing.
- Be of service.
- Find your passion.

I've committed to living all three, daily. The more I grow, the more I can be of service to others, and the more that fuels my passion! Personal growth is a significant part of my annual business expenditure, as I know that my business will only grow as much as I grow. Are you investing in your own personal growth? It may be reading books, attending webinars, taking trainings that teach new skills.

Whatever it is, find ways to continue to grow your knowledge base, stretch your mindset, understand the power of your mind, and the tools that you can learn to ensure you are accessing both your conscious and your unconscious minds for optimal results. Self-Hypnosis is the quickest way to start using both your conscious and unconscious mind together to get the results you want. Self-hypnosis is a powerful way to give suggestions to your unconscious mind in all areas of your life to 100x your success in all areas of our life.

Set yourself up for success by clicking here to see all of my offerings including registering for my next Self-Hypnosis 1 day Masterclass: https://linktr.ee/yourguidedhealthjourney

Use code HEYTAXI to get $100 off my Learn Self Hypnosis 1 Day Masterclass.

Dedicated to my Fur Angels, Duke and Patches, who taught me to slow down, enjoy life more, keep dancing and most importantly, laugh and smile every day.

FROM CORPORATE AMERICA TO CANINES

by JoAnne Dykhuizen

My parents loved dogs and so growing up, I can't remember a time when our house didn't have a dog—a cocker spaniel, collie, German shepherds, silky terriers, and shih zus to name a few. They filled so many happy hours in my life. I still remember the joy and happiness that each dog brought into my life and I firmly believe they all helped in one way or another to shape my interest and passion for animals as I grew older.

But it wasn't until my husband, John, was diagnosed with Multiple Sclerosis (MS) in 1998, when John read that Labrador Retrievers and Golden Retrievers were excellent companions for people with disabilities. I'm sure you know where this is going! So, several days later, we were officially adopted by a 9-1/2-week-old Golden Retriever puppy named Duke who changed our lives forever.

After the loss of John, and having no children and being an only child, Duke helped me in so many ways to fill the void that was in my heart. When I finally went back to work, two weeks after John's death, I remember vividly getting into my car, driving down the driveway and looking at the front window to see Duke looking at me with sadness in his eyes.

To this day, 10 years later, my heart still breaks at the thought of seeing him in the window, leaving him all alone by himself until the pet sitters came to take him for a walk. There wasn't a day that went by that Duke didn't make me laugh or excitedly greeted me when I came home from work. We became even closer than we were before.

As Duke aged, he started experiencing arthritis in his hips and back legs as well as other issues, so I started to do research on arthritis, hip dysplasia, the need for better nutrition and other issues that can occur in senior dogs and read everything I could.

It was then I discovered the incredible value and benefits of canine massage therapy and Reiki not only for senior dogs but all dogs as well. I wanted to give Duke the best possible care as he was reaching his senior years, because he gave me so much love and was an awesome teacher to me. So, I enrolled in a canine massage class and the rest is history.

With Duke's passing, the void in my heart grew larger. Duke was my heart-dog and this was a significant loss for me. Those who have loved and lost a dog(s) know the heartbreak of such a loss.

I had been working at a law firm in downtown Chicago, and after Duke's passing, I became restless and I knew that I had to make a major change in my life. So I left the law firm after 35+

years to pursue my passion of working with dogs on a full-time basis.

Through the knowledge and experience I gained in canine massage school and in my current practice, I was able to discover techniques that helped Duke through the many discomforts he faced, as well as always educating myself on new techniques that can improve my individual client's dog(s) quality of life. I learned what signs to look for, how to do a nose to tail assessment, feel for unusual lumps/bumps on their body and more.

Duke was my inspiration in pursuing a career in canine massage and Reiki. I'm totally convinced that he also helped me with clients in my first year of canine massage, because the majority of the clients he sent me were Golden Retrievers! Hmmm!

I would like to briefly explain my role as a canine massage therapist and why I have the best job in the world.

I often hear from pet owners that petting and canine massage is the same. Although petting is definitely a good and fun thing for you and your dog, canine massage is so much more. As canine massage therapists, we intentionally focus our attention on all aspects of your dog from nose to tail. We examine your dog and look for hot spots, lumps and bumps, how they are walking, noticing if they exhibit any signs of weakness or pain, just to name a few.

I'd like to share with you some information about the value and some of the physical and emotional benefits of canine massage There are numerous physical and emotional benefits of canine massage (too many to mention here) and two stories (of many) that canine massage helped these two dogs:

SOME PHYSICAL BENEFITS OF CANINE MASSAGE:

- Boosts the Immune System.
- Helps to relieve pain and soreness.
- Increases flexibility of muscles and joints.
- Enhances their range of motion.
- Relaxes tired, fatigued, or overworked muscles.

And the one I feel is the most important:

- Promotes early detection of changes that may signal injury or dis-ease.

SOME EMOTIONAL BENEFITS OF CANINE MASSAGE:

- Enhances body awareness and increases self-confidence.
- Promotes positive social development, social skills, and be-havior.
- Lessens anxiety, tension, stress.
- Reduces restlessness and improves quality of sleep.
- Accustoms a dog to touch, and helps him/her develop trust in humans.

Story: A Golden Retriever just finished a nose work session and was stressed out. Nose work is intensive and requires great mental and physical effort for the dog. Therefore, the owner said that it would be difficult for him to relax. Within one minute, the dog was lying on its side and after a few minutes began to relax due to canine massage.

Result: The massage helped relax his overworked muscles which would have tightened up and caused him a lot of discomfort after his activity. It also relieved the stress and anxiety that he had built up during his strenuous activity.

Story: I worked on a male Golden Retriever puppy, who was a puppy mill dog, and was especially reactive to children and a little fearful of adults. I worked with this Golden once a week for 5 weeks. Week One, he wouldn't let me near him. I would toss out treats to him, first from far away and then closer and he would stretch his neck as far as he could for the treats but would never come close to me. Week Two, the owner and I went outside and I didn't pay any attention to him at first. He allowed me to play ball with him, he would retrieve the ball but still didn't come too close.

Week Three, I brought my dog, Patches, with me and we sat on the floor in the living room not paying much attention to the Golden puppy. Out of the corner of my eye, I could see this Golden coming ever so near to where Patches and I sat. Week Four, I sat on the living room floor and he gradually came up to me and let me touch him. Week Five was the breakthrough. He came up to me and let me massage him. I still have the picture of the Golden and I with my arm around him and a tennis ball in his mouth. I'm sure I even see a smile on his face.

Result: The first three sessions required some behavior modification to gain the puppy's trust so I could start to work with him. I was able to gain his trust after the fourth session, and helped him get accustomed to touch. Although the dog still has some slight trust issues around children, he has greatly improved since my initial contact with him and his pet owners have also worked with him to lessen his stress and anxiety and to build his confidence and trust.

As you've heard from the stories above, canine massage can be done in one session (especially relaxation), or it may require several sessions, dependent upon what the certain discomfort your dog is experiencing. Also, each dog is different in their own way and not all outcomes are the same but canine massage can help improve your dog's health and happiness.

Canine massage is also beneficial for athletic dogs (improves performance), dogs recovering from injury (helps alleviate pain before and faster healing after surgery), anxious dogs (reduces stress and increases calmness) and palliative and hospice care (provides compassionate and comfort care for your dog).

All dogs have some form of discomfort in their lives. As a pet owner, a pet rescuer or a prospective new pet mom, my advice for you is that our job is to look for the signs our dogs are giving us. How can you do that? Simply by watching the way they move, the way they sit, the way they lie down. As you spend time focusing on your dog, you will start to notice any subtle changes that may be happening and you can have them addressed right away by your vet.

Dogs have been such a blessing to me throughout my life and have brought such comfort, joy, and laughter to my life. I love speaking and sharing with other pet owners how we can work together with your dog(s) to give them the best quality of life.

Want to know more about what you can do for your dog to create for them a healthy and happier lifestyle while creating a special bond with them and enjoying your time together? For a complete list of the value and benefits that canine massage can do for your dog, check out my website, http://feelsogoodk9massage.com to get more information. Your dog will love you for it!

Looking to start your own business or have just started one and need some suggestions? Here are five successful tips that I've learned throughout my career. I hope you will find them helpful too.

FIVE SUCCESSFUL TIPS FOR STARTING YOUR OWN BUSINESS

1. Congratulations on starting this new journey in your life. How exciting! Take some time to really outline your plans for starting your business. If you are leaving Corporate America, there is a learning curve. Having your own business and being in Corporate America is completely different and it takes some time to adjust to doing things differently.

2. You'll want to work with a financial advisor or accountant to discuss your plans for your business and to get some advice from them on handling the financial plans of your business.

3. Find a good business coach. Business coaches can really help you to move forward with your business. Some business coaches provide individual or group sessions for a fee. Before you make a commitment to a business coach, check out several of them. Most business coaches provide a free consultation call or will invite you to join one of their sessions for free. Make sure you feel comfortable with them

and that you would be a good fit for the type of business that you have.

4. Join one or two networking groups to start. This is a great way to meet new people and build relationships on a personal and business level. You want to find a networking group that will support you in your business. Again, make sure you feel comfortable with the group. Some networking groups charge an annual fee but there are many out there that are free.

5. When you need help with your business because your "to do" list keeps getting longer each day, consider hiring a Virtual Assistant. Virtual Assistant rates vary but you can hire them on a regular basis or for project related activities. They are extremely helpful and will definitely lighten your workload.

Enjoy!

Would love to hear from you!

JoAnne Dykhuizen
Certified Canine Massage Therapist
Owner, Feel So Good Canine Massage, LLC
and Pet Pro for PawTree, Holistic Pet Wellness
jdykhuizen2005@gmail.com
815-341-0919

NOTE: *Canine massage therapists do not diagnose.* If you feel your dog is not feeling well or is injured, you need to contact your veterinarian to have your dog examined immediately.

I help you turn your dream into a reality by building a solid foundation for your business.

READY, SET, LAUNCH—INTO SUCCESS!

by Beth Ann Kaib
Founder of Nomadic Cowgirl, LLC

I am Beth Ann Kaib, a Business Launch Specialist and the owner of *Nomadic Cowgirl*, LLC. I work with aspiring entrepreneurs to turn their dream into reality by building a solid foundation to launch their business.

Have you heard of a serial entrepreneur? That's me. The thrill and excitement of starting a new business fills me with a fire of passion and excitement. It always has. Then the fire extinguisher comes along and all that remains are the mundane daily tasks.

I tried a non-profit service for kids, a multi-level marketing company specializing in vitamins, a makeup company and even a sex toy company to name a few. Despite the variety, my interest diminished shortly after each business reached stabilization.

Though these companies were only successful for as long as the fire burned in my belly and I applied effort towards them, I

deem them successful as the education was priceless. I only define failure by the lack of learning. I learned I loved the business
start-up, just not the business maintenance. A couple of friends
approached me about helping them start their businesses and a
fire was reignited deep inside of me. It didn't take long for me
to realize that I am meant to help others start their businesses
and exceed their business dreams. I finally figured out why I was
placed on this earth.

You are probably wondering what a *Nomadic Cowgirl* has to do
with business start-up. I wanted a name that was both mem-
orable and reflects all that I embody. After the exit of an abusive marriage, I did what any sane single mom with a physically
disabled teenager would do. I bought a travel trailer and refur-
bished it before taking it across the nation and back a couple of
times.

Nomadic Cowgirl was born on this journey. As for the Cowgirl
portion, I was born and raised in Western New York where I
grew up riding horses. In my adult life, prior to my nomadic
journey, I specialized in incorporating horses into therapy sessions with special needs children.

A recent college graduate with some experience in a broken
healthcare system and zero knowledge of building a business,
decided to solve the recurring problem that was breaking her
heart. She started the process to open her own therapy clinic
and sensory gym where the focus was on the family learning how
to best help the special needs child from a holistic standpoint.

The new owner's husband found me...the rare unicorn with a
background in Occupational Therapy turned into a Business
Launch Specialist. I was hired to build a website for the new

pediatric Occupational Therapy clinic on the other side of the country. I did not know I was about to help launch an empire.

With some helpful guidance in building a solid foundation, the result surpassed a dream come true. Within the first five months she maxed out her caseload and hired three new employees. The set expectation was to hire the first employee in 12 months. The impact she had on the families she served surpassed her wildest dreams. Not to mention capturing the attention of local media and a national Occupational Therapy organization in the process. She now plans to expand with several locations into her neighboring state, with me by her side.

TIP #1 - PHONE AND EMAIL

One of the biggest heartbreaks I see is business owners setting up and launching their business with a personal phone number and email address. What happens when your business grows and you want to hire an office manager or you want to take a vacation?

There are so many cheap alternatives. You can look into apps that provide a second phone number on your existing phone to preserve your peace and avoid carrying a second (or third) phone. Google allows free email creation with a gmail.com address. Another option is to invest in Google Workspace and create your domain email for greater professionalism at a low monthly cost. This also provides a Google My Business page, online Drive storage, video calls, a YouTube channel and more, when done correctly.

TIP #2 – PROFESSIONAL PHOTOS

Whether you are selling products or a service, professional photos are a must. A good headshot that captures the best angle and lighting with a professional touch up goes a long way. Family photos, filters, and selfies do not. A professional photographer's perspective can ultimately enhance the visual appeal of your products and set you apart from your competition.

The investment of professional photos demonstrates your level of professionalism, provides greater online trust, and increases the customers confidence in your company. Be sure to ask your photographer how many revisions you are allowed and if a release to use the finished products for promotional materials is included.

TIP #3 – CHOOSE YOUR PLATFORMS WISELY

When starting up a business, you are full of motivation and want to do it all. That doesn't mean you should. Most likely, you don't belong on **EVERY** social media and business review platform out there. Do your homework to find your target audience and where they are spending their time. That's where you want to invest your resources.

Pinterest is great for the right business, but is it worth you creating five posts a day to play in the game? Is your crowd a younger generation hanging out on TikTok and Instagram Reels? Maybe the professionals on LinkedIn are a great match for your service?

Please understand that I am not saying you should be on only one social media or business review platform. I'm recommending that you allocate your time and resources appropriately according to where your target demographic is.

TIP #4 - PROTECT YOUR TIME

As you embark on your newest adventure, you are probably balancing a steady income and/or a family at the same time. It's easy to get lost in your To Do lists with everything that needs attention at work, around the house, and for your family.

Don't forget to include mandatory self-care time in your weekly schedule. Whether it's a daily walk without your phone, an hour at the gym, a pedicure, or date night...schedule the time and do it. No excuses! You can't successfully grow or run a business on auto-pilot or burn out mode. Your business, your health, and your family will all suffer the consequences of you not putting yourself first.

TIP #5 - STREAMLINE & AUTOMATE AS MUCH AS POSSIBLE

Based on my client's reviews, the biggest area I help entrepreneurs with is streamlining and automating. I get to know you, your business, what's working, and what is not. Understanding your future business dreams and current limitations is vital to increasing your efficiency.

Once I have a solid understanding, I help you automate and streamline as much as possible. Whether it is automating your website and appointments or streamlining your onboarding process and digital communications, you will be able to focus more time in your area of expertise and with those you love. A fresh perspective allows you to reset and view your business procedures in a whole new light. It may even inspire a new business idea!

Nomadic Cowgirl has been one of the biggest blessings of my life. I have met so many amazing people through my business adventures and developed some lifelong relationships. I have learned more about coffee, Brazilian butt lifts, towing, polygraphs, real estate, and modern art than I ever dreamed possible. The list and my knowledge base is constantly growing. Nothing is more rewarding than developing these relationships and helping people push past their self-limiting beliefs into greater business success than they could have ever imagined for themselves.

I have a special offer just for you! Visit www.allthingsbeth.com/offer to receive a complimentary business audit or strategy session. Your choice!

If you have been in business a while and wondering if you need to update your image, take advantage of new technology, or improve your intake process, the business audit is for you.

Haven't started your business yet? That's okay! We can have a forty-five minute in depth conversation about your business dreams, current business reality, and strategize your way into success.

To my sons who have saved my life more than once. You keep me grounded and make me happy and hopeful on this ever changing planet.

And to my parents: I miss you both. I am grateful you continue to guide me from the great beyond. Thank you, thank you, thank you.

I SPOKE UP AND ENDED UP AWOMANUP

by Traci Hill

There was a knocking at our door that was so loud it echoed through the stairways and hallways of our four-level, 3000+ square foot brownstone. Peeking through curtains I saw several shiny black SUVs like the ones used by POTUS security . We must be getting a visit from Barack himself! Do they have the wrong house? Is my (then)-husband and father of my elementary school-aged children in the Secret Service? Ahh, this is why he has been so dayum secretive!

Pounding continued. I got another angle and saw huge men dressed in black donning vests with MARSHALL on their backs, guns on their waists, and badges dangling from chains around their necks. What the friggidy fuck is going on?!? I headed towards the door and am stopped by my husband who whispers, "Trae, don't go to the door! I heard one say something about arresting someone. Don't know what you did but I will not allow them to take you!" "Whah? Arrest me?" I naively scanned my memory for any offense I may have committed. DC is serious about getting their parking ticket revenue but I paid my tickets! Think, Traci, think! Is this my wild teen years coming back to haunt me? Did my father, who recently went on to be with the Lord, and whose multi-million-dollar estate I managed, end up in hell and the poe poe think I am in on some kind of scam?

My husband obviously wanted to protect me but we could only hold up there for so long. I could not put my kids through this. I couldn't let them see me taken away in handcuffs doing a perp walk down a busy Washington, DC thoroughfare. I directed my husband to take the boys to school allowing me to write them farewell letters before being escorted to the Big House. They left. Almost immediately, I got a call on my cell, "This is Traci," I answered. "Ma'am, we have your kids and your husband." I panicked and started hyperventilating! I **CANNOT** believe they are holding my family hostage to get **ME**! My college "chemical experiments" are fucking with my memory! **WHAT. DID. I. DO?**

Hugging my unsecured triple Ds, I ran to see my baby daddy being arrested! Gurl, you got to be fucking kidding me! **THIS** asshole knew he was wanted and had me thinking I was the fugitive! I knew right then and there I was divorcing that mother fucker who, because of his white-collar financial crimes, I started to refer to as "Mini Madoff".

CUT! And end scene.

Before the curtain hit the stage, I realized that my ass was duped! This mofo sold himself to me as this successful money managin', financial firm havin', family carin' southern gentleman! So **THIS**, ladies, is when I decided to vet everyone and everything that impacted my life and my children's lives. I also knew from then on I had to pay attention to the status of the deals I made. In this case, my marriage was a deal I made with "Mini Madoff" and I **ASSUMED** he was doing what he agreed to do in our marriage. I trusted him, but didn't verify his financial position– lesson learned!

When I manage a work team, I have weekly 1-on-1s with each team member. I analyze the office numbers to make sure we're on track for their success **AND** mine. We have semi-annual reviews where we are all evaluated and can make changes and ensure we are on track with what we were hired to and more importantly **AGREED** to do. Why didn't I do this at home? Short weekly meetings and quarterly finance meetings to make sure we, as a family, were on track to pay our children's college tuition, pay off the house, be able to retire on time and without having to eat canned cat food under the tarp where we sleep, pee and "home" school our children!

I also knew I needed to have another revenue stream and not to rely on just one. When they took that @&$#+%{{]\+%%\|¥•]¥] away, I lost a source of revenue. I was in shock, and so afraid about how I was going to maintain the life to which my children had become accustomed. After scanning my brain, I had an Oprah **AHH HAA** moment! I decided to start charging for the previously pro bono professional development coaching sessions that leveled up people's careers. I launched *AWOMANUP* with the mission to ignite HER confidence, accelerate **HER** path, and level up **HER** lifestyle.

At *AWOMANUP*, I facilitate professional development opportunities that encourage women to amplify their voices on all of life's stages, because we know that a woman has the power to alter **HER** circumstances. This is **MY** mission statement as we teach others what we learn from our own life experiences.

As you now know, I didn't always charge for coaching services. I was "paying it forward" by sharing what I learned over decades of working, studying, on-the-job training, both my successes and my failures. The information and experience was not free to me, so why should others assume that it is free to them. But the key was my recognizing how valuable my knowledge was. I came to demand that those who could afford to pay for impromptu "so Traci, what would you do in this situation" conversations pay for this life-changing information. Keep in mind, those impromptu sessions ultimately guided them to promotions and raises that on average increased their annual compensation by tens of thousands of dollars!

Today, ten years after my divorce and launching *AWOMANUP*, I am in a better place financially but **NOWHERE** near where I should be because I did not require fair compensation for my advice or financial disclosure and stability in my marriage. Back in the day, I had been downsized, had contracts end abruptly, and could rely on Mini for subsidy in lean times. Now I know I am my own financial safety net and it demands that I get paid what I am worth.

I also learned the hard way that all kind acts are not reciprocated. Not that I sought a tit-for-tat payback, but maybe a show of appreciation to recognize my generosity when I needed a lil' help. I have a close sista-friend who says I always see the good and the potential in people; that I spent too many of my resources helping others and many times to my detriment. I was naïve enough to think people were kind and had a moral or professional compass similar to mine. But what I do know now for "true true" (as they say in the bayou) is that what I thought wasn't "true true." Not all people have a giving spirit or just weren't indoctrinated to be mindful of the reciprocity needed in relationships. I also learned that pain and poverty (I have experienced both) are excellent motivators.

OK ladies, what have we learned from my not recognizing, amplifying, and charging for my worth? We learned that everyone has to pay for the value of proximity to strategic partnerships. Reciprocation is key. I learned to demand a negotiated and/or agreed-to fee in exchange for the commencement of work. Otherwise, no services or goods will be delivered. Period. When a prospective client wavers, instead of turning into "captain save a hoe", I just nicely say, "It was a pleasure speaking with you, please call me once you've made a decision." Peeps need to pay a fair price for what they want to **RECEIVE**. If they want to pay less, then they have to be satisfied with getting less. Remember your worth and demand no less from your clients (and partners).

HERE ARE MY LEVEL UP TIPS :

1. **Sometimes we need help figuring out our worth until we build up that muscle memory.**

   One of the first things I ask my clients to do when they are interested in a promotion or leveling up their career, is to make a list of every single thing they do on a daily basis. No two days are the same. My job description doesn't define or dictate what I **CONTRIBUTE** (highlight these all-cap words, sis). My talent, my desires, my hopes, my dreams, my love for what I do for a **LIVING**, (because we gotta live and living ain't free) or the partner I love, influences the work I put in. If we're invested in a relationship (work or personal), we women usually give much more than the "job" description requires.

2. Women especially struggle with amplifying their worth.

If you are like many of my clients who have trouble making their list, it's ok. Our female indoctrination doesn't encourage being braggadocios, so we have to dig deep to take deep breaths, call a friend, reread our newly formatted resume, and get the courage to play the "I'm worth it" game.

Here's a "true true" I've experienced a zillion times in my years of negotiating compensation packages. Men have less problems making their lists or amplifying their experience, and they seldom need to be reminded of their own worth. Quick statistical fact: men readily apply for jobs they are not 100% qualified for. They sell themselves up to the opportunity because they are confident in their capabilities (sometimes ridiculously confident!). Women, for the most part, won't even apply for the position if they don't have everything listed on the job posting.

3. You need to "Man-Up."

What does this mean for you? This means, in many cases, you're definitely not selling yourself **UP** during your reviews or when talking to your significant others, reminding people, as often as needed, of your **WORTH**. I shared the need to own your **CONTRIBUTION** and demand the need to have reciprocation. Hence *AWOMAN-UP*. We women have to "**MAN UP**"! It's too easy to burn out if you're not properly compensated. One day you're gonna get fired, want to quit, or you will become preoccupied with the lack of balance, and **YOUR BRAND**, **REPUTATION**, and **PASSION** (and relationship) will suffer. And, ladies, that's all we got!

4. **Do your research.**

When negotiating your compensation package, don't take it personally. This is about being your own advocate at work or at home. You need to know the prospective company or life partner can provide what they're offering. You must do the background work to understand their financial position. You need to know if their offer is something they can sustain or even deliver in the first place. There are lots of websites, articles, etc. that will give you the information you need. For your personal relationships, there are databases and all criminal records are public. I did not research "Mini Madoff" and got straight-up ripped off, and a lot of his shiggidy was a Google search away. If you're talking about the person you're gonna be lying in bed next to you might want to get that Social Security number, know how they stand in the community, look at that credit score and those bank accounts. Heck, I would love to see a month's worth of mail coming to their house or place of business. Are there cut-off notices? Are they paying vendors timely? Are the prospective company's or life partner's liabilities much more than their assets? Are they meeting payroll or child support?

Not knowing this information, leads to some hard ass lessons and a lot of money lost, tears shed, and time wasted. There are holes I'm still climbing out of because I didn't do my due diligence. I know it can be hard to say no or goodbye, but the net gain is considerably higher than the losses.

5. **Know that everyone offers a solution!**

You are a solution for your partner. The solution can consist of giving a much-needed hug, a shoulder to cry on, sex or a well-dressed travel companion. We're solutions for the companies we work for. Even if you're in the mail room, somebody needs to sort the mail. That's a problem that the company needs to solve and they're willing to pay $40,000 a year to have their mail sorted. That's a contract that's solidified when you agreed to work there, and it needs to minimally be fulfilled and preferably you exceed the expectations of a mail sorter. Any opportunity agreed to, is an opportunity to shine and grow.

Remember, you are a limited liability company (LLC) which is a privately held, **LIMITED** company. You are not an **UN**-limited source. All wells run dry eventually, especially if dipped and sipped out of too much. If there is no rain (**PAYMENT**) to compensate for what was drank, it hastens the dry'ness and I know no woman wants their well to be dry. Remember, you control what goes in your p*ssy and your purse (a shameless and appropriate plug of my forthcoming best-selling book, *Your P*ssy, Your Purse...You Control What Goes in Them* #SpeakItIntoExistence).

So, let's sum this up because I have only one chapter in this wonderful advice-filled book. Figure out your worth. Remember your worth. Amplify your worth. Charge and get paid accordingly. It is **ALL** business at the end of the day and there is no shame in a fair exchange.

Lastly, allow me to offer a well-known example of learning your worth, amplifying your worth, and then being compensated accordingly for said hard-earned worth...

1978: Tina Turner left Ike's ass. She was 39 years old and only wanted her name. She knew her name's worth.

1985: After seven hard and penniless years later, '85 was the year of her comeback concert. It was during those years of pushing through her doubts and fears, supported by close friends and others who also knew and **INVESTED** in her worth, **AND** were subsequently **PAID** for said support, she met her husband. She was 46. Knowing her worth, putting in the hard work, and hustle, were outwardly confirmed. Her courage attracted opportunities and her soul mate.

1994: Tina insured those fabulously iconic legs for $3.2 million cuz she knew those legs were worth a fortune!

Today Tina Turner has a net worth of $250 million and she owns every cent of her worth!

Moral... know your worth! If you are having trouble remembering that...

Take these 2 Steps forward:

1. Take the *AWOMANUP Am I worthy* assessment

2. Schedule a call with me to talk about your results *How worthy do I think I am*

You need to know you are worthy! Understanding how to amplify your voice will give you the courage to be paid what your skills and love are worth.

No matter the results, you can be *AWOMANUP* to LevelingUP

Live your life without regrets!

BLOW UP THE BOX

by Julie Jones

On my entrepreneurial journey, I was often told to "think outside the box." In the early stages of my journey, I decided pretty quickly to "blow up the box" for a number of reasons.

First, even though I served as a police officer for ten years in the State of Wisconsin, I may have enforced law; however, I, myself, am a rule breaker. I don't fit in the box. I am authentic and true to who I am, and I don't live in comparison or bow to anyone's expectations.

Second, I see people living their lives as if they were "six feet under" in a box, running the hamster wheel of life, exhausted, overwhelmed, and stressed. I saw first-hand, when I was a police officer, how quickly life can change. Here today and gone tomorrow. There is no promise of tomorrow, so I live each day as if it were my last. I am grateful, every day, when I wake up six feet above ground.

Finally, I know mindset is so important in the journey of being an entrepreneur. There can be so many setbacks along the way that you begin to question why you even started this journey to begin with.

Trust me, I have had those days where I have sobbed uncontrollably because of self-sabotaging fears. Therefore, I avoid the "idiot" box as it is often called ... yes, the television set. I have not watched the news in over ten years for it is filled with negativity and dire situations which are sure to create an outlook of doom and gloom. Trust me on this one. Stop watching the news and reading the newspaper. Those two actions alone will have a huge impact on your mindset.

What do I mean by "blowing up the box"? In my journey as a speaker and adventure coach, I can proudly say I am like no other. I wear googly eyeglasses and I am often seen wearing costumes for the holidays. Actually, life is to be celebrated every day, so my tribe never knows how I may show up. I inspire joy in overwhelmed, overworked, and chaotic individuals by focusing on what you "get to do" rather than what you "have to do," so you can live a life without regrets.

What would your life look like if you started saying "YES" to spontaneous opportunities and saying "NO" to what puts you on the hamster wheel of life? It may sound crazy; however, my clients live more in the moment, have more fun, and have the freedom to fully express who they are.

Please don't misunderstand. My journey has not been all rainbows, unicorns, and sunshine. I lost my mom 19 years ago at the early age of 59 when she passed from early onset Alzheimer's. My dad passed away from undiagnosed pancreatic cancer a little over three years ago. My husband had a massive seizure in front of me on November 6th, 2021, and had to be resuscitated right in front of me by paramedics. Thankfully, he survived.

The aforementioned tragedies are my strong "why" that drives me to make an impact and difference through my speaking and coaching. What I do has a ripple effect for the client and for everyone they come into contact with in their life. I have a goal to leave people better off for meeting me even if for just a short time. It may be with a simple smile or eye contact to know that I see them. A hello or kind word will go a long way in today's world.

One of my clients, who I will refer to as "John" came to me because of his fears and what he refers to as mind talk. He had convinced himself that he was not good enough, that he was stupid, not deserving of good things in life, and overall, struggling with self-esteem and self-confidence. John had recently broken up with his fiancé, was struggling at work, and his relationships with his family were strained.

As you read this, does some of this sound familiar? I know my mind talk has been horrible at times. Do you ever stop and think about what you say to yourself? Imagine if you said those same words to another human being. Stop it! You are enough. Every one of you reading this book has an important message to share that can only be heard from you. I encourage you to be loud and be proud in the pursuit of what sets your heart afire.

Over the course of a few months, as John and I worked together, his life began to shift. When I start with a client, I tell them that I am going to give them the best information I have to give. I certainly don't know everything. I walk the walk and talk the talk. It is then up to the client to decide whether or not they implement and take action on my promptings.

John took action in a massive way. He started to "high five" himself in the mirror. Thanks Mel Robbins for that tip! I asked him to make a list of things he was tolerating in his life. John realized that list was long, and his home was not a reflection of the "new" John. When he changed some of the items in his house that he had been tolerating, his self-esteem started to skyrocket.

John was going to be seeing his family when he went out of town, and he knew he wanted to improve the relationships. We reframed some old thought processes, and during his visit with family, I received a message.

Here is what he wrote:

> *"I just had a powerful conversation with my mom and brother, specifically my brother. It was very positive and will move our relationship forward. Thank you for helping me gain the courage to speak up."*

Actually, John, you have had the courage all along. You just took my coaching and applied it in your life. You did the hard part.

I share this client's story because it's important to have people in our life who believe in us before we have the belief in ourselves. I know this firsthand. Even though I was a police officer and SWAT member, when it came to launching my business and following my passion for helping people, the fear would take over. There were so many times that I didn't believe I was capable or courageous enough to follow my dreams.

When it comes to your life and your business, here are some ways to "blow up the box" that I have implemented in my own journey.

1. **Follow the joy!** What makes you truly happy? What could you do for 24/7 within your business that doesn't seem like work? Now, I am not advocating that you work 24/7, and whatever sparks your joy, it should also be creating income for you. If you have a hard time with this, go back to when you were five-years-old. What did you love to do? I loved to play teacher which is why I now "teach" through speaking and coaching.

2. **Say YES to life opportunities.** When I set my goals for 2022, nowhere on my list was the idea to produce my own television show. Yet, that is exactly what I did in 2022. I produced my own show, Stop Waiting Start Living, on the Zondra Network. Let's be honest, I had NO IDEA what I was doing or why I even said yes to the idea. I figured it out along the way, and it has given me a platform to reach even more people. Remember the ripple effect? I am excited to see how this journey progresses.

3. **Create your own opportunities.** Again, armed with a "can do" attitude, I created, from nothing, a two-day live event where I had 50 people in attendance. I heard that when Tony Robbins had his first live event, three people showed up. To say I was proud of myself is an understatement. During that event, I truly was in my zone of genius and I had the time of my life during the event. If you want to be on stage, create your own! Remember, people are waiting for you and your message.

4. **Start eliminating your "toleration" list.** Seriously, make a list of what you are tolerating from small items to big items. Funny as it is, I was tolerating this dining room table that was clunky. Every time I walked past it, I would mumble about how I hated it in my dining room. It's actually a beautiful table that is designed more to be outside than inside. Once I got the new table in my dining room, my self-esteem sky rocketed. I am worthy enough to have a beautiful table. Recently, during a holiday dinner, I received so many compliments on the table and chairs. What are you tolerating? You already have a mental list. Write it down and start making changes.

5. **Most of all, HAVE MORE FUN!** I already shared how I wear crazy glasses and costumes. For the month of December, I wear an elf outfit every day, yes every day! Now that may not be your style to wear costumes; however, there are simple things you can do. Swing on the swings at a playground, run through a water fountain, wear a superhero cape for the day, stand outside a store and hand out flowers, sing as loud as you can in the shower, tell corny jokes. Fun makes everything better and will create the ripple effect within the most important business.....the business of life and love!

My website is juliejones.biz

I dedicate this writing to those who have helped me understand and optimize my health.

DNA -YOUR WAY TO OPTIMAL HEALTH

by Patty Lach Daigle

Courageous Transformation is not something everyone strives to attain. But when your heart and life are not satisfied with the current situation, create the life that inspires you and helps you reach your highest potential.

I came from a coastal town in central New Jersey. Both of my parents were factory workers. My mother worked very long hours and the money she made helped us have the extras we would not have had such as clothing and holiday gifts for my sister and I. My father's income put the roof over our head and food on the table.

I was an average student in school, and very active in sports my entire childhood. I graduated with seven varsity letters, something I am still very proud of today. But despite my athletic skills, college was considered out of the question. My father told me that he could not send me to college because he just could not afford it and my grades did not warrant it. So my options after high school graduation were limited. I would ride my bike to the beach almost every day as it is my happy place and one day I found myself riding to the military recruiting station. The recruiter talked me into taking the military entry exam and three months later I was sworn into the U.S. Air Force. That began my twenty-year military career.

My Air Force career and eleven years of civil service helped me with intangible qualities like leadership, comradery, discipline and determination and they are perhaps the most rewarding of all my military benefits. Eleven years into my military career, I became a single mom with financial struggles; I couldn't afford daycare. This is when I was introduced to network marketing and started my own business. Little did I know where using this income model and the opportunity to create a business that is purpose-driven would take me and where I would end up today.

Now what? I was sixty and retired! I was told that sixty is the new forty. There was still a lot of life in me and I was not one to sit around watching TV. Back to the network marketing side hustle! In the past, it helped provide me with the cash flow I needed to pay for daycare, to meet new people in the community, to expand my horizons and help me grow from the introverted comfort zone I was living in. At 60 and beyond, it is something I have embraced to this day. Even at the age of sixty-four, when you come out of your comfort zone and follow your passion, magical things happen.

I am thankful to the people who I have had the opportunity to follow and learn from in the network marketing industry. The entrepreneurs who have followed their dreams, carved their roadways to success, and continue to lead others to accomplish their dreams. Even with this inspiration, I'll be honest, my transformation has not been easy.

Why did I start my current business? I had lost 30 pounds in 6 months and no medical doctor could tell me why. I learned about Epigenetic DNA testing and Nutrigenomic DNA testing and this was the start of my getting healing results! I quickly became interested in the exact same holistic medical care which has saved my life. I felt I finally found health and wellness providers who care about my quality of life and helped me to get on the road to recovery.

What I discovered from the DNA testing was that I needed to be detoxed! A parasite was discovered in every organ of my body. EBV and Candida were running rampant at the same time. Not to mention the damage from the required vaccines from my many years in the military. I was one unhealthy person on the inside. Also, it was discovered that I had vaccine damage from a TDap vaccine which made me a Type 1 diabetic. Basically, I learned that my body was shutting down.

I was told a change in my diet due to the inflammation some foods were causing was imminent. No more nightshades, high histamine foods or gluten. A four-month detox, tracked by a professional holistic health doctor, started me on a new journey of health and wellness.

Thank you to the holistic doctors who I have met through my current network marketing business. They found imbalances in my skeletomuscular system, toxins in my body, nutritional deficits, and unresolved "negative emotional blocks", beliefs and perceptions which were adding to my sickness. And they could help!

It was now time for me to get to work learning to read labels on food packages. Removing sugars, lowering carbs, and pre-packaged foods has made eating a challenge. I have become a research guru, looking up all ingredients not familiar to me. Including labels on toothpaste, mouthwash, shampoos, and all the daily, routine, health products. Protecting my health comes first now and it is my passion to help others make the same commitment. **MY LESSON FOR YOU: CHOOSE TO CARE FOR YOURSELF!**

Even three years ago, my capacity, strength, and wisdom were just not where they needed to be to allow me to live a life of purpose and leave a legacy. But, the pandemic offered me time to stay home and learn to connect to and utilize the upgraded technologies of social media. My own personal growth became a necessity. This is when I started searching for books I needed to read and to find the leaders in network marketing and health & wellness, all to take me to another level. I learned to search for groups on Facebook with common interests and started meeting "my" people. I have continued to follow those who give me the opportunity to Choose To Win and continue to add value to my betterment!

Yes, my new education comes with a cost; financial and time. But when you find a passion and really feel it is how you want to help others, you bite the bullet. You make the decision to replace the bad habits, to strengthen the qualities you want to develop in yourself to achieve your desires, dreams, and goals faster. You find the time and you find the money.

So you may ask, what makes my business unique because there are quite a few health and wellness businesses out in the marketplace. I offer Full Circle health knowledge and choices for your wellness. I have found trusted, quality businesses that provide me with the full circle of products to help my customers/clients. Just one did not do it all, so I have branded myself as *YourDailyNourishment* and incorporated each one of them into helping others look and feel their optimal best. Let's start with the Nutrigenomics DNA Testing.

Nutrigenomics testing identifies a patient's genetic protein variations to identify sites of metabolic weakness. These key proteins are involved in signaling pathways in the cell, enzyme conversion and nutritional delivery. Subsequently, this can be used to determine naturally occurring chemical agents in food that could prevent the onset of diseases such as obesity, type-2 diabetes and other diseases. The testing company also offers the next generation of custom nutrition based on your own-one-of-a-kind DNA. Yes, nutrition is compounded specifically for your body as there is evidence that suggests people metabolize carbs, protein, and fats differently based on their genetic makeup.

Next, we all want to increase our human performance in sports, work and life. Nutrition just isn't always the answer. If you could have a drug-free, 100% non- invasive solution to human performance, would you listen to the person offering those solutions? Whether you're looking to be more active or move with athletic power and precision, there is a line of natural products that can help you reach and surpass your goals.

Another wellness line I recommend is designed to give you pain relief and to give you better mobility, helping you live a happier, healthier and more active life. Known as Human Performance Technology, products rely on the science of vibrotactile stimulation. When the technology is in contact with the skin, the micro-vibrations trigger a response in the brainstem, helping to improve a person's pain, balance, mobility, or a multitude of other ailments and discomforts. Each pattern works with a different neural network; they can also work together at the same time producing: **WHOLE BODY WELLNESS.** Contact with it triggers a neural response in the brainstem that helps manage pain, as well as improve mobility and balance. **WHOLE BODY WELLNESS:** The brain and nervous system processes that provide stimulation and a waterfall of wellness responses happen, from more energy to enhanced balance and quality of life.

Last, is the line of health products that got me started. With potential benefits of better-quality sleep, boosted vitality, enhanced physical energy, and mental clarity plus healthy weight management support, you gain a state of balance and optimal function. My biggest recommendation is a combined healthy diet and daily exercise. Since I have a stronghold on labels, this line holds steadfast in being Organic | Vegan | Kosher | Sugar-Free | Non-GMO | No Gluten, Soy, Whey or Dairy and Informed Sports Certified.

Presence of the *Informed Sport Certification* quality mark on product packaging demonstrates to athletes and consumers that every batch of a product has been tested for more than 250 substances prohibited in sport and that the product was made in an environment with quality systems appropriate for the stringent demands of sports nutrition manufacturing.

Cellular fitness does not end on the inside. Your skin is the largest organ of the body. The skin and its derivatives (hair, nails, sweat and oil glands) make up the integumentary system. Skin care is the last of what I help with. The line is produced by one of the largest manufacturers in the world and the products all contain Dead Sea mud, salts or minerals. All the minerals in Dead Sea salt not only boost hydration but also reduce inflammation.

This doesn't just help relax you, it also helps hydrate dry skin brought on by skin conditions. One of the worst effects of these conditions is itchy skin.

Of course, besides my reliance on the products and systems that have transformed my own health, you get my own experience, guidance and belief to help you attain your own health goals. What is better than working with someone who has shared your same health and wellness challenges and is living proof of what is possible when you commit to your own self-care and wellness. It is my passion and purpose to help as many people as possible through the most current science-based health and wellness products to live happier, healthier, and longer lives.

WONDERING HOW TO TAKE ACTION TO GET HEALTHIER TODAY?

1. **Take care of you.** Drink more water, exercise, walk, yoga, meditate, stretch, and/or move your body for at least 30 minutes every day. If you want things to change, you have to change yourself from the inside out.

2. **Create your coat of armor** to protect your mind, body and soul. Give yourself permission to be the healthiest version of you. Build a positive support network; we choose who to keep in our community.

3. **Develop an Attitude of Gratitude.** The feeling of thankfulness rather than living a life of being ungrateful, critical, and unappreciative.

4. **Have you ever wondered what your genes say about your diet?** Take advantage of today's science and have a DNA Nutrigenomic test accomplished. Learn about your DNA and how you can be the healthiest version of you!

If you want to get started on your journey to health, here is my calendar, check in for your complimentary 30-minute strategy appointment.

https://calendly.com/yourdailynourishment/30min

My offer to you, when you purchase the $199 DNA health kit, I will reimburse you $50 as a thank you.

For Kayla & Lindsay, I love you both with all my heart! And to my friends & family who helped me along this journey (many more so than you realize) - Thank You!!

CREATE YOUR HAPPYNESS

by Kathy Starr

TIME TO TAKE ACTION

It wasn't that the light bulb went on ... that happened many years ago.

It was that the light switch finally got flipped!!

It just happened. I was finally ready, and even excited about it!! Everything was aligning and falling into place.

My mindset was finally there. I can't say any one thing that finally flipped the switch from thinking about it, to doing it, to taking action. It just did.

A couple things happened in the six months prior to the switch being flipped, that really gave me the confidence to push myself forward with my entrepreneurial dreams. But even then, I still had to push myself to do them, and make them happen.

I committed to write a chapter for this book. It was an exciting big step, but also scary. I intentionally told some friends and family, so I couldn't back out. Plus it made it "real" for me in my mind. Wow, I was really going to do this—write a chapter in a book for women entrepreneurs! I also referred a longtime friend Traci as a fellow author to the publisher. We had fun, a lot of laughs, and motivated each other as we each wrote our own chapter. The thought of being a published author helped build my confidence and sense of value that I had something to say and share with the world. I could do this!

I invested money into and hired a highly-recommended trademark attorney to register a trademark for my branding, *"Create Your Happyness"*. I had already secured the domain names several years prior, when I came up with the idea. The trademark was a lot of money for me, and it was scary. I had to force myself to commit and hit "send" for the attorney and related fees. However, I knew it was wise to ensure the registration process was done correctly, including a thorough risk analysis. But I was excited and I pushed myself to take that huge step!!

While planning my business the past couple years, I had strategized a new professional last name, which would be easy to say, spell and remember, convey positivity, and help brand myself and my business. I also researched job titles I wanted to use, which would quickly communicate what I offer to prospects and others. I tried them out at networking events, which strengthened my confidence, mindset and excitement. It was empowering seeing them in writing on my nametag and elsewhere, and alongside my now-TM-registered company name:

Kathy Starr, Health & Wealth Coach
CEO & Founder, *Create Your Happyness*

Most importantly, I contacted Jennifer, one of the top global income earners for the direct sales health and wellness company I had partnered with several years ago. I was honored last summer when Jennifer offered to help me build my business when I was ready. However, I literally had to force myself to hit the "send" button when I messaged her a couple months later. I knew by contacting her, I was committing to taking significant, full-time action to build my business and make it a success. This was a good thing, but it was scary, and a big step for me. Although it felt great when I did it!

Jennifer recommended I attend our company's New Year Kick-off Conference. It was sold out, but she found a ticket and hotel room for me. A week later, I flew to the Conference! It was invaluable in meeting like-minded, positive, healthy, successful, inspirational entrepreneurs and leaders with our company. Plus excellent product, coaching, sales, and business training.

MY JOURNEY

Going back several years, my journey to becoming an entrepreneur was long. From the time I was introduced to my health and wellness company, I knew building a business in network marketing with my health and wellness company was my best opportunity for a successful new career and new life in my late 40's. I shared the products with some clients along the way, but was stuck regarding building my business full-time into the success I knew it could be.

I knew building a successful business and helping others lead healthy and wealthy lives could enable me to live the affluent lifestyle I had worked for, sacrificed for, and been accustomed to in supporting my former husband's career. But I struggled forcing myself to do so. Going through a difficult and painful divorce had taken a hit on my self-esteem and self-confidence, so embracing being a successful entrepreneur was even harder.

In the 23 years we were together, my husband and I moved 10 times in 5 states, had two girls, and raised them far from any family support. It was a lot. I worked full-time in marketing for the first half of our marriage, while he got his MBA at night. I left the corporate world to start a business I had thought about for many years. However, I never got to it, as soon after that we moved out-of-state again, life got in the way, we moved again (& again), and I worked as a stay-at-home-mom, which I admit, I did enjoy. All of the moves were very difficult on our kids, marriage, and family. Plus, as he rose up the career ladder my own career became non-existent.

I had loved my husband and our family, and thought we were a team, both committed to building and supporting our life together. My two girls were in high school during the divorce. Within 2 years, they had both left for college, and I went through the empty nest stage, a hard time for most parents, even harder when you are going through it alone.

Now in my late 40's, I realized I had always done everything for everyone else and neglected to focus on myself. I could take action for others but had blocks and was stuck regarding taking action for myself and my own dreams and well-being. Thankfully I started using a "superfood" nutrition program soon after the divorce, and still use it daily. Taking care of my own health was essential as I was healing. Fueling my body and mind, I felt better and lost over 25 lbs and kept it off for over a year. I was within 5 lbs of the weight I'd been in my twenties! The products tasted great, and were affordable and convenient. I was proud of my weight-loss accomplishment, and looked better in my 50's than I had in my 30's and 40's. I had replaced my unhealthy eating habits with a long-term healthy lifestyle, and it also helped my mindset and confidence.

My brand, *Create Your Happyness*, was born in 2016, when I realized it was what I was learning to do myself, after the unexpected major detour in my life. I got my domain names (so exciting!!), and kept going on my healing journey.

I learned a lot, and grew a lot, along the way. Sometimes it was slow. It was often difficult and took courage to keep trying. I discovered new activities and places, met new people, and figured out how to create a (new) happiness for myself.

I also discovered in my late 40's I have ADD. This filled in a lot of puzzle pieces for me and I wish I'd known in my teens or twenties. I believe my life, career, marriage and relationships would have been very different if I'd been diagnosed earlier, but the knowledge itself was enlightening. I struggle with the ADD traits of perfectionism, focus, motivation, procrastination, and others. ADD is under-diagnosed for women. If you think ADD may be holding you back in life and as an entrepreneur, check out ADDitude.org for helpful resources.

PIVOT TO RESULTS

"Change your thoughts and you change your world." Choose to change your thoughts when they are not serving your well-being. This phrase was invaluable to me as I healed and worked on my mindset. I have shared this with many friends, and when I was struggling, I would write it on a sticky note and put one in my car, on my mirror, etc.

I knew I had a lot to share from my own journey as a health and wellness coach to help others. Occasionally others tried to dissuade me from my vision and dreams. I was figuring out what I wanted in life, versus what others wanted for me. All along, I knew my health and wellness company was ultimately best for me, and what I wanted to do. I just didn't know all the pieces yet. That took a while.

I had to confirm the vision and direction I wanted to convey with my brand, *Create Your Happyness*. I knew it included positive, healthy living, as when you feel good in mind and body, you can accomplish a lot more every day.

Choose your hard! I was a reluctant entrepreneur initially, and I think it's part of why I was stuck and not ready for so long. I knew that after being out of the corporate workforce so long, my alternative was to go back to a cubicle and work 50+ hours/week for someone probably half my age. And still never get to the 6-figure life I'd been accustomed to before the divorce. I knew it would be much smarter to work hard for myself and my own dreams, and take advantage of the much better opportunities with my health and wellness company, building my own business.

But my mindset was still stuck, and I had to force myself to do it.

I had to get myself in the right mindset to build a business. If you have trauma, you have to heal. It takes a lot of work and patience. Although I don't think I'll ever be 100% healed, I have many of the pieces to move forward now, and I am ready!

Once I flipped the switch and made the choice to commit to myself and creating my happiness, I attracted clients looking for the same. By forcing myself to take action, the pieces fell into place, giving me the confidence and the self-worth that my insights and support are valuable. I could do this!

I realized my healing journey was similar to what many of my coaching clients in my health and wellness business experience. It often takes them a long time to get in the right mindset and commit to losing weight, changing poor eating habits, getting healthy, and then maintaining a healthy lifestyle. Many times they must heal from traumas which led to their being stuck in a self-destructive cycle. Sometimes it takes them decades, and they are always "getting ready to get ready" (e.g. "I'll start my diet next week").

When they commit in their mind, invest in their well-being and health financially, and follow my health and wellness company's scientifically-proven system that works, my coaching clients are successful in maintaining a healthy lifestyle. Whether their goal is to lose weight, get healthy, or even earn extra income, their mindsets are key components for success. With my ADD challenges, I understand that what is easy for one person, may not be easy for another person.

I took many big and little steps on the winding path to building my business. The pieces finally came together. Now I'm ready to take the stairs, and I'm even excited for my adventure to the top. I know the view will be beautiful along the way, including as I help others create their happyness!

SUCCESS TIPS TO HELP YOU GET IN THE RIGHT MINDSET:

1. **Find** and contact a successful mentor and ask them to guide you to help you succeed.

2. **Commit** to your mentor you are coachable and will work hard and consistently for your success.

3. **Join** an Accountability Group with like-minded go-getters to motivate, educate, and share resources with you, and hold you accountable to your tasks and goals.

4. **Invest** a financial commitment in your business. An amount that is significant to you, that you would not want to lose. Be accountable to yourself as well!

5. **Prioritize** yourself and your business. Practice good self-care and be healthy.

By healing, and taking action on these items, I had flipped the light switch on, and I was finally ready. I was excited to commit full-time to my business, and make it a success, while also helping my clients achieve their health and wealth goals.

Create YOUR Happyness! To create a life you can't wait to wake up to, contact me today, and let's make your health and wealth goals & dreams happen for you.

To our success, let's go!

Kathy Starr

> *I dedicate my chapter to my family who are always there to back my act.*

FIVE THINGS THAT AFFECT HOW YOU PRICE YOUR COACHING SERVICES

by Lil Barcaski

I n this chapter, I want to talk about something near and dear to my heart... **MAKING MONEY!**

I meet many people who are in the coaching field who have the best hearts, minds, and spirits. But too often, they are not getting paid what they want or need to continue to serve their clients.

When I first started the business I am in now, I too had this problem. I didn't know my worth. I saw other people who had been writing much longer, who knew more about publishing than I did and who were charging astronomical amounts and I thought, I can't compete with them. I need to be "cheap." But in time, I started to gain confidence... and clients. I got some great coaching. I did lots of research. I learned new skills and became adept at the ins and outs of publishing books as well as writing them. I added services. I added staff. The company grew... and grew.

I had been a self-starting entrepreneur for most of my life. In the past, I've been a successful restaurateur and professional actor/musician. I have learned a lot from the many "lives" I have led. I've worked in major hotels cooking, serving, and ultimately managing large staffs. I have played music in front of hundreds of people. I even had a speaking role in a major motion picture. I have always had to put myself out there despite the fact (something most people would be floored to know) that I am and always have been extremely shy. As a kid, I barely spoke in class. It took me till sophomore year of high school to find my tribe and ultimately, my voice.

Most of the work I have done in my life has included learning to use what I like to call the seventh sense—the sense of urgency. Whether it is cooking for hundreds of people, making sure that every event in the hotel was running smoothly simultaneously, or even performing in front of large crowds, I have learned that things happen fast. Life happens fast. You need to be able to roll with the punches, correct the mistakes on the fly, think on your feet.

Mostly, you have to show up and be visible. I've never stopped learning and training and I think that no matter what your coaching style is, you have to continue to grow and you can't hide.

For the last 15 years, it's been my pleasure to be the CEO and project manager of GWN Publishing/Virtual Creatives, a publishing and marketing firm based in Tampa Bay. I am also a ghostwriter and consultant and have ghostwritten dozens of books in the business, memoir, and even fiction genres.

While I love writing, editing, and publishing books, I have a desire to see people leave careers they are growing tired of and step into their entrepreneurial journey, especially women over 50 who have a lot more to do, more to give, and more to experience. To that end, I have written a book and course coming out soon called, *Entrepreneurship 101: Your Guidebook to Success.*

One of the things I think it's most important for every entrepreneur to know is how to position themselves when it comes to charging clients. Let's talk about five things that will help when pricing your services.

1. UNDERSTANDING THE VALUE OF THE SERVICE YOU OFFER

Your time is valuable, but when you talk about the value of your services, you have to consider your training, experience, and education. If what you offer is mostly time and talent based, you must take into account the years of study, time in the field, courses you've taken, work you've done with other people, apprenticeships, and time spent giving away your services to build a reputation.

When you sell a product, you need to consider how much to retail that product for. Retail stores buy wholesale. They get the products they sell at about 40 to 50 percent of the cost. Basically, they double the price. But they take the chance of buying dozens, sometimes hundreds of pieces of each SKU. What happens when not all those products sell? They put them on sale of course, and consumers grab them up. But retail shops have rent, salaries, utilities, and more to consider. So that 50% profit becomes 20%, if all goes well.

When you are selling coaching services, your costs are not in buying goods, but rather, mostly in your time. That time will include, preparation, time spent creating course materials, marketing, creating sales funnels. All those things take time even before you meet with a client for coaching.

How do you determine the value of your services? One way to determine how to price your coaching service is to compare the pricing of other people doing something similar to what you're doing. This doesn't mean you need to beat their price or try to undercut them, but it's good to know what your competition are getting for similar services. What is the hourly rate you feel you are worth? How do you consider your hourly rate when putting coaching packages together?

Consider the type of coaching you want to do. For this, we help you create a Money Triangle. The bottom of the triangle is your least expensive offering and will take up the least amount of your time. That could be as simple as a once a month (or week if you're ambitious) zoom meeting that you charge $19 to attend. People can ask questions, share their problems, and have you, the expert, offer sage advice. It could also be an online course that you simply create once and market with no other participation from you (money while you sleep). With those, you will "upsell" to the next layer of the triangle. For example, this could be a 90-day, group coaching program for $497 or a 6-month for $997. Those numbers go up with the years of experience you gain.

The top of the triangle is where your one-on-one or private clients live. This is where the bigger money is made. At this level, the client will pay for your personal, undivided attention. This can be 6 months or a year and often clients will renew. The cost here can vary from as little as $10,000 for a year to as much as $100,000 for a month. Where you fit on that scale, is something you need to research, and soul search.

2. GETTING OUT OF YOUR OWN WAY

Most entrepreneurs are not born, they're built. They come to entrepreneurship sideways. Most of us go to school, probably college or beyond, and take a job in the field we studied. There are some people who have the entrepreneurial spirit from birth. They were the ones who took the lemonade stand seriously, found ways to make extra money after school, started small businesses in college, even created new software or invented new products. But that is not typical.

Most of us entrepreneurs realize we don't like working for someone else. We hear about an opportunity to start a home-based business, we learn about a coaching program that speaks to what we want to do for other people, we have the burning desire to write a book and speak about our experiences or expertise, and we become consultants and coaches.

But, sometimes, you get in your own way. Transitioning from a career to entrepreneurship is scary. You lose confidence too easily. You spend hours doing discovery calls with potential clients just to hear, "This a bad time," "I just can't afford you," or "It's not really what I need right now but I'll keep you in mind."

UGH! Rejection, stinks! So, you start to self-doubt.

Am I good enough? Is what I'm offering something anyone wants? Am I kidding myself that I can be a coach?

Everyone goes through this. Writers call this, the dark night of the soul. Once a book is finally completed, here is the pattern:

Wow, this is great! I am a genius. I will win a Pulitzer for this book.

A week later upon rereading...

This is a terrible book. I'm an idiot. No one will like this. I suck!

Two weeks after that...

You know, this is good. I'm a really good writer. People will like this book.

The same pattern happens with new business owners and coaches, sometimes even with people who have been at it for years. If you hold on long enough, the dark night of the soul settles down, and you begin to realize that you're going to be fine. Confidence wins the day.

3. BEING NEW DOESN'T MEAN FREE

Free is not a solution to getting clients. Yes, there will be people that beta test your course, read your book, come to a free webinar and give honest feedback. However, if you are constantly offering coaching without being paid, you're a charity not a business. Another big mistake new coaches make is giving too much free advice on discovery calls. If you solve a person's problems in an hour on a free call, why would they want to come to you for coaching? Listen to their issues, offer a nugget, and then suggest they consider a group you coach, or a course you offer, perhaps go right for one-on-one coaching packages.

4. YOU BRING YOUR OWN MONEY ISSUES TO THE PARTY

Lots of people starting a new business are on a budget. Some are downright broke. That is not the best position to be in when starting a business of any kind. Your money issues are yours. Making an assumption about what a potential client can or cannot afford is a common mistake. When you're nervous about money, asking someone else for some feels like climbing a mountain. You let your nervousness about money affect your ability to ask for what you're worth.

When the conversation turns to talking about price, try making no assumptions about what the person you're talking to can or will want to pay. Instead, come from a place of knowing that your service is a game changer for that person. You are offering to serve them something that will help them, possibly change their lives. That is invaluable. Assume they can afford you and it's going to be a yes. Remember, you're solving, not selling!

5. YOUR MARKETING IS WRONG

Identify your ideal client or what we call your avatar before you create a marketing plan. Direct your marketing towards the person who will be ready and able to work with you, who understands the value you bring, and who wants to take action. You will save yourself a lot of wasted time and effort.

One coach spent nearly three hours on a call with someone she assumed was a potential client. At the end, when she made the ask, the person divulged that they could not afford her. Had she been clear about the cost much earlier on, she would have been able to end that conversation and could have recommended different options or a reference to someone else for that person.

We helped this same coach hone her messaging and create a marketing plan that targeted the right type of client. Then she met with a different client for about 20 minutes whose reaction was, "Great! Sign me up!"

She closed the sale with a 20-minute presentation based on learning how to ask for the sale and what language to use to express what she could do for the client.

"I'm only looking to work with people who want to take action, who want to be successful in their businesses. If you feel that's you, then I would love to work with you."

Realistically, it takes depth of experience to be a coach. It requires time to get to those 10,000 hours that makes you an expert in your field.

> **NOTE:** The concept that if you do anything for 10,000 hours that will make you an expert was popularized by Malcolm Gladwell's blockbuster book "Outliers." As Gladwell tells it, the rule goes like this: it takes 10,000 hours of intensive practice to achieve mastery of complex skills and materials, like playing the violin. If you

do the math, 10,000 hours equals less than 5 years of 40-hour work weeks. Not as daunting when you think of it that way.

You have to find your depth and seek ways to acquire experiences. Education is key, but so is working with a coach.

All coaches need a coach.

Even if you have all the tools in the world, they don't matter unless you know how to use them. That's where a coach can teach you how to sharpen the tools in your toolbox and how to gain more of them.

If you would like that kind of powerful assistance, book a discovery call with me:

https://calendly.com/liltheghost

I also invite you to join my Facebook group – The Entrepreneur's Success Club. Introduce yourself and share about what you do. https://www.facebook.com/groups/701800384355888

For my strong, brilliant, beautiful daughter, Poppy, you are the inspiration for who I am today.

WHY YOU NEVER WANT TO BE THE SMARTEST WOMAN IN THE ROOM

by Jill Knerr

ABOUT ME

I always knew I was smart and resilient. Maybe I did not put it into those exact terms, but I knew from the praise I received from my parents and the feedback from my teachers, I was SMART! My resilience is based on my surviving a dysfunctional and abusive childhood to become who I am today – a strong woman, a committed mother, a woman who supports the wellbeing and success of other women, and a confident entrepreneur.

I moved out of my family home at 17. My mother passed away when I was 12, my sister had gone off to college and, being left with only an alcoholic father. I decided I was better off on my own. Was it easy to take a minimum wage job and pay my bills until I went to college? Not at all. But some of my best life training and ability to come back from hardship came from that year working odd jobs to help fund my college education. I worked as a deli manager and even took a temporary position working on an automobile air filter factory line – third shift from 10 pm to 6 am.

Talk about an experience! I met a group of women who loved their families and worked very hard for very little to support them. I too worked very hard and showed up on time for every third shift – and you know what? This tight-knit group of women, who were initially dismissive and cold towards me as "that college girl", soon realized I was one of them. They saw that I was working my butt off to survive, plus I was on my own. In just 4 weeks I am still proud to share that I moved from assembling shipping boxes (the lowest level job on the line) to the front of the line wearing the huge oven mitts and breaking the air filters out of the molten hot metal casts – and that assembly line belt moved **FAST**! Even as a short-timer, I was invited to attend the farewell party this bonded group of "overnighters" hosted to commemorate the final shift together after the company decided to end the overnight shift. To this day, their stamp of approval of me means so much. And looking back, perhaps this was the start of my realizing the power of the support and cheerleading of other women.

Next I attended a very small liberal arts college and worked full-time during the school year. Again, I had to buy my own gas, pay my car insurance and all other daily essentials. I was very lucky to have an on-campus position as a resident assistant and received grants that covered basically one full year of tuition. But I still left college in 1995 with over $27,000 of college debt. So, I know how it feels to start out in life "behind the eight ball" when it comes to financial position. Being a smart, hard-working woman, I proceeded to get my first administrative assistant position at a D.C. non-profit. Then over the next 28 years, just like at the factory, worked my way up – from job to job, company to company—to today being a C-Suite Executive focused on operations, administration, finance, and strategic planning. Nowhere along this path did I choose a job or career that fed my soul, but it has continued to fill my bank account and provide the stability my childhood was missing, which is very important based on what I will share next...

Let's talk about my 41st birthday, a very pivotal time in my life. Only two days prior, I found out my husband wanted a divorce. I had become very codependent in my marriage and only hung out with other moms and we focused on our children when we met up or talked. I had no family to turn to and had no network of close friends to look to for support.

Luckily, around six months after my separation, I met a group of women who were involved in direct sales—and their welcoming, supportive, positive community inspired me to consider new possibilities for my life and my future. When I would find myself stuck in VICTIM mode, forgetting about my bad-ass ability to work hard and move ahead, these women reminded me that I was capable of anything I set my sights on.

MY ENTREPRENEURIAL JOURNEY

I did launch my own business and ended up learning how to leverage my home-based business and its related expenses to lower the taxes on my W2 job. It created financial stability for me and my daughter as we transitioned into a single income, single parent household. Along with my business, my new friends encouraged me to work on myself. I dove into personal growth trainings and retreats and can happily share that today, ten years after my 41st birthday, I am a completely new woman. I am still single but in a happy, long-term, healthy and fulfilling relationship with a man who I feel is my best friend and my equal/partner. I have grown my income to be not only financially independent but also to have the extra money to invest in funding my retirement and my daughter's college education. And would I be here today if I had not embraced the friendship and mentorship of other women? No way!

During the pandemic, I finally dove in and co-founded a business to support other women in creating, building, and scaling their own purpose-driven businesses. *Hey Taxi* was born from a shared passion with my partner, Dawn Cermak (a successful serial entrepreneur herself!), to pour belief into other women who want to do more with their lives as well as share our hard-won combined 50+ years of experience to help them with the business side of things. Yes, the tax strategies are in there, but also the business plan, the financial strategy, and the network of other female entrepreneurs to provide their own lessons learned and guidance to each other. Being able to build my own powerhouse network of *Hey Taxi* women who focus on servant leadership, giving back, and supporting other women in their own success, is the realization of the path I have been on since I was 17.

HOW DO I CONTINUE TO LEVEL UP MY GAME

Now, if you are like me, you may often feel that your networking groups or communities for entrepreneurs fall short of your expectations and needs. Maybe you have more experience and success than your current network. Or find that you are so excited to openly share your resources and knowledge while others sit back and take notes versus contributing. So how do you find a tribe to help **YOU** level up? I was on this quest in 2022 and discovered an amazing resource for C-Suite professional women called "Chief". It had an application and interview process so all participants were vetted both for experience level and for their commitment to support the other women in their monthly meetings.

When I attended my first session, I was hooked. I actually was **IN THE ROOM** with such impressive women with amazing careers and we were engaging both as colleagues and friends. I was able to add value for the other women, but also to learn so much— from career path strategies to how to set boundaries and take the needed time to spend quality time with my family.

We talked about everything in our lives—and found such great similarities as well as impactful differences. We were from different age groups and ethnicities and our backgrounds were all over the place. The diversity of this group challenged me in new ways and also helped me think and BE outside the box in my life and my business. Being in Chief continues to serve me on so many levels.

My Chief experience made me start thinking... How can I create this for my fellow female entrepreneurs? What parts of this community and network for women in the Corporate world would easily translate for business owners and how could I develop a like-mentoring and support group for us? I know so many entrepreneurs operate in a silo due to their own workload in running a business. There is immense value in taking the time to connect with women you know, like, trust and respect to receive valuable feedback on your pricing, programs, courses, branding, etc. It can save you time, money, and sanity to have the honest opinions and guidance from other smart successful entrepreneurs.

MY PASSION PROJECT

Well, let me introduce you to the *Hey Taxi Peer Advisory Board* (PAB)! We have created a networking/mentoring/support peer group for women running their own businesses. Each PAB cohort is limited to eight women for an eight month program. And, yes, we have an application process to ensure you are in "the right room" with women who will challenge your ideas and help you step outside your comfort zone to increase your business profitability and profile. These peer groups focus on addressing each other's current challenges, supporting Big Goals, providing **CRUCIAL** accountability, helping to identify key referrals, and making connections for your business growth. The PAB cohorts convene monthly to make sure there is a consistency to the interaction and communication with your peers. Each cohort meeting is moderated by me or my co-founder to provide structure and ensure every member has the opportunity to maximize their participation. I speak from experience—you do not have to do this alone!

I owe my success to the generosity, inspiration, and mentorship of other women. Perhaps it is because I lacked a mother figure from age 12-on, but only in looking back do I now recognize how important a role strong women have played in my life. From the hardworking and loyal South Carolina factory workers to the positive and embracing community of network marketers to the inspiring and impressive women of Chief, each one has left me a better person in their own unique way. So, it only makes sense that my contribution to my peers would be to provide a safe space with vetted participants who are committed to each other's success. The Peer Advisory Board is my gift to every woman who is ready to take the next big step in her business, but needs the guidance and belief of other strong women to help her take the leap of faith.

MY 5 SUCCESS TIPS FOR FEMALE ENTREPRENEURS

1. **SEEK OUT MENTORS** and experts that can challenge the status quo in your business.

2. **EVERYONE NEEDS ACCOUNTABILITY!** Whatever you do, find someone who will check in with you regularly to keep you on track and on task with your goals.

3. **NEVER UNDERESTIMATE** your own knowledge, skills, abilities, and life lessons that will continue to drive your success.

4. **VALUE YOUR PEERS:** the women who are on the same entrepreneurial journey as yourself. You do not have to build your business in a silo. If you connect with other purpose-driven entrepreneurs, they will always have your back.

5. **YOUR NETWORK IS YOUR NET WORTH** – truly! Always save the contact information and follow up with new connections in a meaningful way. You never know how the person you meet today can impact your success down the road.

DAWN CERMAK

Dawn Cermak has been an entrepreneur for 33 years and is currently building businesses 9, 10 and 11! She did not set out to be an entrepreneur, it happened purely by accident, but she is eternally grateful that it **DID** happen—as it has allowed her to create a life of total time and financial freedom and to live abroad in Barcelona and London with her children, while working her businesses. She is now an International Speaker and also appears frequently on Summits and Podcasts. Dawn's mission, in all of her businesses, is to be a beacon for women to have the tools, the belief, and the financial means to design a life that truly delights them!

Her first business was in database management and her second business, and many of her early businesses, were in the field of Special Events! Her sister/partner took care of the creative side, and she did the "CEO" stuff... and learned by **DOING**! She also "fell into" Network Marketing and is a multiple seven figure earner with a health and wellness company. Surrounded by so many other "Accidental Entrepreneurs" in that field, she saw a huge need for business and tax education, in order for those entrepreneurs to maximize the profitability of their businesses, and, with her partner Jill, founded *Hey Taxi* in June 2020. She is passionate about supporting female entrepreneurs on their journey, and empowering them to live the life of their dreams!

JILL KNERR

 **Jill Knerr** has spent the past 27 years overseeing and supporting operations, administrative, finance, and human resource functions of non-profit organizations and currently serves as the Chief Administrative Officer at a D.C. metro non-profit financial services association.

In 2020, Jill co-founded *Hey Taxi*, a business supporting mission-driven female entrepreneurs with the business tools, training, and resources to help them build profitable legacy businesses. In 2023, *Hey Taxi* is launching The Entrepreneurs' Business School to provide online, on-demand business education for women as well as Peer Advisory Boards to connect high-level entrepreneurs with their peers for strategic guidance and exchange of best practices with other entrepreneurial thought-leaders.

Jill is a member of Chief, an international private membership network focused on connecting and supporting women executive leaders. She also co-hosts a monthly professional women's networking group, Wine, Women and Worth, based in Howard County, MD.

www.ingramcontent.com/pod-product-compliance
Lightning Source LLC
Chambersburg PA
CBHW050447150626
46551CB00029B/1977